MW00678161

Chronicles of Intimacy

Kelli Penn

Published by Steven Lester, dba MindShift Publications

Atlanta, GA

ISBN: 978-0-9899590-7-0

Printed in the United States of America

TABLE OF CONTENTS

SECTION THREE:
CHRONICLES OF INTIMACY

SECTION FOUR:
TASTE AND SEE

Introduction:

You're Invited to the Table

How do I begin to chronicle a fifty year love affair with my LORD? How do I begin to tell you Who I have found Him to be? How do I use mere human words to describe the peace that floods my soul when I just whisper, "FATHER?" How do I describe what it is to call on Him as FATHER, KING, GOD, SHEPHERD, BRIDEGROOM, REDEEMER, SAVIOR, PARACLETE, COMFORTER, GUIDE, TEACHER,...... ? How do I express the mountains of fear that melt away as I begin to declare His Names, His Character, His AWE .... the holy exhale experienced as GOD gives GOD. Quite honestly, I don't know where to begin. I told Him that as I sat here and stared at this blank page. And yet, I need for you, those I love so dearly, to know that there is so much MORE than what you see. I need to leave something that challenges you to not miss the whole point of being on this earth. I so desperately want to introduce you to the LOVER OF MY SOUL.... and the POINT OF IT ALL.

This book was written primarily for my family, especially for my beloved children and grandchildren. I wanted to be sure I reminded you and pointed you to what I so desperately wanted my life to yell... that He is REAL and WORTHY and SO WORTH ALL. This book is also written for my little children and grandchildren in the faith. You are the children, now fully grown, I had the absolute honor of teaching in class, children's church, or chapel. You became one of mine when I had the privilege of teaching you, and I ache for you to know and weep when I see you struggle. Finally, this book is written for the truly hungry who dare to believe there is more to life than what we see. You are right!

Just so we are clear, I am no super-Christian. Oh my, anyone who really knows me will tell you that on any given day I begin the day as one big wad of anxiety, fear, control, performance, selfishness,... well the list is getting long and a bit embarrassing. By the end of this book, you will be thoroughly convinced that I am the strongest weak person you have ever met.... looking so strong (and bossy) and yet truly one step away from hiding to have a breakdown. I brought nothing to the table of my relationship with the LORD but an ache...and that is where the mystery began to unfold. Time after time after time, I came with my racing mind, trembling hands, unanswered questions, and preconceived opinions... and GOD... GOD gave GOD... and I exhaled. And my hope for this book? My hope is that an ache will awaken in you, the ones I love. I pray it will be an ache so strong it brings a disillusionment with this world, a distaste for empty religion, and a realization of your own weakness. I pray it will be an ache that brings you to His table each day with your nothing. I get excited just thinking about it. For I know WHO you will meet at that table. I know what HE will bring. I know the joy you will find at that table. Prepare to be AWEd, prepare to be loved, prepare to be comforted, prepare to be seen, prepare to be transformed... every day. Prepare to once again finally exhale....

1 Corinthians 2:1-9

"And when I came to you, brethren, I did not come with superiority of speech or of wisdom, proclaiming to you the testimony of God. For I determined to know nothing among you except Jesus Christ, and Him crucified. I was with you in weakness and in fear and in much trembling, and my message and my preaching were not in persuasive words of wisdom, but in demonstration of the Spirit and of power, so that your faith would not rest on the wisdom of men, but on the power of God. Yet we do speak wisdom among those who are mature; a wisdom, however, not of this age nor of the rulers of this age, who are passing away; but we speak God's wisdom in a mystery, the hidden wisdom which God predestined before the ages to our glory; the wisdom which none of the rulers of this age has understood; for if they understood it they would not have crucified the Lord of glory; but just as it is written, 'Things which eye has not seen and ear has not heard, and which have not entered the heart of man, all that God has prepared for those who love Him.'"

SECTION ONE:

Come Magnify the LORD with Me

Psalm 34:1-3-

"I will bless the Lord at all times; His praise shall contin-
ually be in my mouth. My soul will make its boast in the
Lord; The humble will hear it and rejoice. <u>O magnify the</u>
<u>Lord with me, and let us exalt His name together</u>."

Chapter One:

Have we lost our AWE?

Since my heart in writing this book is to speak to my children and grandchildren (and all my children and grandchildren in the faith), I really feel I must start with an apology. I think my generation failed your generation in fully sharing with you the character of GOD. You see, many of us grew up at a time where GOD was often portrayed as harsh. When we had our "grace awakening" and realized GOD loved us, we were determined to introduce our children to the love of GOD. Let me say here that I pray my life oozes the reality of the all encompassing, life changing, there just aren't enough words... LOVE of GOD. So why do I feel a need to apologize? I apologize because I fear in our eagerness to be sure you didn't miss the intimacy of GOD, we failed to share with you the infinity of GOD. Have no doubt, GOD is INTIMATE. He knows how many hairs are on your head, calls you by name, and longs to have a personal relationship with you. But that intimacy loses all of its magnitude if you fail to recognize that GOD is INFINITE. He is the GREAT I AM and He is SO

MUCH MORE than us. I fear in our zeal to make GOD personal to you we unknowingly robbed you of the gift of AWE.

A.W. Tozer said, "What comes into our minds when we think about God is the most important thing about us."[1] Our view of GOD impacts EVERYTHING... how we view ourselves, how we view each other, how we view the world, how we live our lives, how we spend money, what we watch, what we listen to, the friends we choose...everything. And most importantly, how we view GOD impacts how we interact with Him and has the potential to revolutionize and give true meaning to our life or to rob us of our entire reason for being.

When you truly love someone, you can hardly bear for that one to be misrepresented ... especially when that ONE is the LOVING GOD OF THE UNIVERSE. In the absence of AWE, current "trends" in viewing my BELOVED just make me hurt because they rob Him of the glory He deserves and because they are robbing so many I love from experiencing an encounter with the ONE TRUE GOD. Satan loves to offer a counterfeit for truth, and AWE is no different. Here are three of the lies/views that I see deceiving so many, especially the young. AWE is replaced by...

- AWW...Isn't GOD sweet?- This is a view of GOD as a really good buddy who winks at my sins and gives me everything I want. This perspective leads us to approach GOD flippantly and selfishly as if He is just a little more than us but quite able to be manipulated by our charms. This view of GOD dismisses His MAGNIFICENCE and His IN-COMPREHENSIBLE OMNIPOTENCE, and it robs us of His AWESOMENESS, His HOLINESS, and His SOVEREIGNTY.

We forget to be amazed by the enormity!

- UGH...Isn't GOD scary, hard, angry, or worse yet terribly boring? Isn't He against... well everything? This perspective generally leads to one of two hideouts. Some try to mostly stay clear of GOD and hope they don't get noticed or associated with Him because who wants to be seen as a judgmental hater. Some choose the other hideout and twist themselves in knots trying to appear perfect and harshly demanding the same of everyone else. This view of GOD dismisses His LAVISH LOVE, His TRUE COMPASSION, and His FAITHFULNESS, and it robs us of experiencing His MERCY, His GRACE, and the favor of His CLOSENESS. We forget to be wonderstruck by the love!

- EHH...Why does GOD really matter? Isn't He... ancient, just for old or weak people, not really relevant for today, just for Sundays? This perspective leads us to usually just ignore GOD. We may go to church if we are pressured, but it is something we do to be with or to appease people. When it comes to GOD, we are apathetically disengaged. This view of GOD dismisses His PERSONALNESS, His NEARNESS, and His ACTIVE ENGAGEMENT, and it robs us of experiencing His AMAZING WITH-NESS, His DIRECTION, and His PEACE. We forget to be enraptured by the presence!

Oh my beloved ones, can you hear me crying, "Nooooo! Don't buy the lies! Don't be deceived! My PRECIOUS LORD, our

GREAT REDEEMER is SO MUCH MORE." For if you settle for these crumbs, you will miss the true BREAD OF LIFE who desires to meet you and feed you every day of your life. You will miss the LIVING WATER that truly satisfies over and over and over again. You will miss HIM!

In John 10:10, our dear JESUS says, "The thief comes only to kill and steal and destroy; I came that they may have life, and have it abundantly."

Why am I so passionate about revealing these false views? I am passionate because I love you so very much, and because these wrong views threaten to kill your joy, steal your passion, and destroy your purpose. But JESUS offers LIFE ... ABUNDANT OVERFLOWING LIFE. LIFE is Who He is and all He offers... every single day and in every single season!. Can I encourage you to stand in awe?

A few years ago, I was meditating on the idea of AWE. As a teacher of children (and because I am a child myself), the LORD gave me an acronym to help me grasp the idea of "AWE." I hope this helps you:

A- Amazed by the enormity of His character (Amazed by how BIG He is)

W- Wonderstruck by the beauty of His ways (Wowed by how KIND He is)

E- Enraptured by the reality of His presence (Excited by how REAL and PRESENT He is)

Consider this a plea for you to dare to AWE. Let's explore these ideas a little further in the next few chapters.

(By the way, if you are wondering what AWE has to do with intimacy, here is the deal. You can't be truly intimate with someone you don't truly know, and you can't truly know GOD without AWE.)

Important note: Throughout the book, you will notice names and characteristics that are written in all capital letters. Take special note of those descriptors. The key purpose for writing this book is to share what I have found to be the secret to ... everything... hope, peace, truth, life... everything. The secret is the character of our GOD. The all in capital letters words are a few of the characteristics WORTHY OF ALL PRAISE GOD has revealed Himself to be to me in our times together. If you just read those characteristics and embrace them as true in your life, the purpose of this book has been fulfilled. These few characteristics I am sharing with you leave me speechless, but as Job says in **Job 26:14,** *"Behold, these are the fringes of His ways..."* In other words, He is SO MUCH MORE... and He wants to bestow Himself on you. WOW!

> **Psalm 33:8-11**
> *"Let all the earth fear the Lord; Let all the inhabitants of the world stand in awe of Him. For He spoke, and it was done; He commanded, and it stood fast. The Lord nullifies the counsel of the nations; He frustrates the plans of the peoples. The counsel of the Lord stands forever, The plans of His heart from generation to generation."*

Chapter Two:

Amazed by the Enormity of His Character (Amazed by how BIG He is)

How do you use mere human words to describe the INCOMPREHENSIBLE HOLINESS of ALMIGHTY GOD? HOLY... meaning... other than, sacred, set apart, consecrated, worthy of great reverence and respect... or to keep it simple... NOT LIKE US and SO MUCH MORE AWESOME and WORTHY OF REVERENCE than any other.

In Isaiah 6:3, the angels declare He is HOLY, HOLY, HOLY.

Three times ...with the number three in scripture meaning completeness. The angels are declaring HOLY GOD to be COMPLETELY AND PERFECTLY SET APART/ MORE AWESOME. That alone makes Him... WOW... but Isaiah's encounter holds so much more. Let's look closer at the encounter in Isaiah 6:

vs. 1–
"In the year of King Uzziah's death, I saw the Lord sitting

> *on a throne, lofty and exalted, with the train of His robe*
> *filling the temple."*

Oh the imagery of this verse alone! For in this scene, we see our GOD as KING ON THE THRONE OF HEAVEN, REIGNING, SOVEREIGN, SO MUCH HIGHER, MAJESTY. But there is more. Notice the train of His robe. In ancient times the length of the train of a king's robe signified how powerful that king was known to be. Notice the train of our GREAT KING. His train actually fills the temple. Imagine layer after layer of that robe filling from floor to ceiling. OUR SOVEREIGN RULER is ALL POWERFUL, MORE THAN ABLE, CONQUEROR.

vs. 2-4-

> *"Seraphim stood above Him, each having six wings: with two*
> *he covered his face, and with two he covered his feet, and with*
> *two he flew. And one called out to another and said, 'Holy,*
> *Holy, Holy, is the Lord of hosts. The whole earth is full of His*
> *glory.' And the foundations of the thresholds trembled at the*
> *voice of him who called out, while the temple was filling with*
> *smoke."*

My beloved ones, can you even fathom this scene as Isaiah took in the sights and sounds and presence of heaven? Here is the LORD OF HOSTS, the RULER OF ANGEL ARMIES, the FOCUS OF ANGELIC ADORATION. Angels are flying, foundations are trembling, smoke is filling the place, praise is ringing! Let's not forget that the angels mentioned that the whole earth is filled with His glory. GLORY...ahh, His GLORY. Glory means WEIGHT, SPLENDOR, GREATNESS. The angels said the whole earth is full of His GLORY.

Well, dear ones, that only makes sense for He is the ONE TRUE CREATOR of the whole earth (and the heavens for that matter). He is the MOST AMAZING ARTIST designing every season, every sunset, every species, every star in the sky. And speaking of stars...

Psalm 147:4 says,
"He counts the number of the stars; He gives names to all of them."

Do you have any idea how many stars there are in our galaxy alone... and do you have any idea how many galaxies there are in the universe? Well, He knows how many there are because after all, He named each one! He is the MASTER CREATOR and GREATLY ATTENTIVE TO DETAIL.

He is the MASTER ARCHITECT designing gravity, placing the sun far enough away from earth for us not to burn to death and close enough for us not to freeze to death. And have you looked at how He built the human body? The GREAT DESIGNER gave us bodies that grow, move, reproduce, compensate, and heal. He very specifically and intentionally designed you just as you are and knew you before you were... you. Psalm 139:13-18 says He is the WEAVER IN THE WOMB, FORMER OF INWARD PARTS, WORKER OF WONDERFUL, KNOWER OF MY FRAME, HOLDER OF MY DAYS, SKILLFUL DESIGNER...shall I go on? And this is just in reference to His design of you. (By the way, it also says you are "fearfully and wonderfully made.") The whole earth is full of His GLORY... well I should say so!

Now let's get back to Isaiah. How did he respond to this amazing revelation of the ENORMITY of our GOD? Was His view, "Aww, isn't God sweet?" or "Ugh, isn't God scary, hard, angry, or worse yet terribly boring?" or "Ehh, why does God really matter? Isn't He... ancient, just for old or weak people, not really relevant for today, just for Sundays?" What was Isaiah's viewpoint after the curtain was pulled back and he caught a glimpse of GOD? Notice I said.. glimpse. How did Isaiah's peek at the enormity of GOD impact his life?

vs. 5-7-

"Then I said, 'Woe is me, for I am ruined! Because I am a man of unclean lips, and I live among a people of unclean lips; For my eyes have seen the King, the Lord of hosts.' Then one of the seraphim flew to me with a burning coal in his hand, which he had taken from the altar with tongs. He touched my mouth with it and said, 'Behold, this has touched your lips; and your iniquity is taken away and your sin is forgiven.'"

Quite honestly, Isaiah was just... undone... with this glimpse of GOD...fully and utterly undone. He was all but speechless and deeply broken because in light of this encounter his descriptive words and the words of all those he knew just seemed...unclean. He was AWEstruck with the enormity of GOD and in light of that enormity, Isaiah was fully done with himself and quite honestly done with everyone else. This is where you just have to love GOD! For in this moment of broken surrender, GOD shows Himself as CLEANSER, REDEEMER, FORGIVENESS, GRACIOUS, TOUCHER OF THE BROKEN PLACE, PROVIDER OF THE HEALING TOUCH,

RESTORER OF PURPOSE, EQUIPPER... I could go on and on. He reaches out to Isaiah to reconcile them. Wow! How did Isaiah respond to the AWESOME GOD WHO CAN'T BE CONTROLLED, the GRACIOUS GOD WHO ADDRESSES AND HEALS OUR BROKEN CONDITION, the GREAT I AM? Did he dismiss, hide from, or ignore God's greatness?

vs.8-
"Then I heard the voice of the Lord, saying, 'Whom shall I send, and who will go for Us?' Then I said, 'Here am I. Send me!'"

Following Isaiah's amazement at the enormity of GOD, He encountered the GOD WHO CALLS, the TRINITY WHO INVITES PARTICIPATION, and the ONE WORTHY OF MY ALL. How did he respond? It is almost like Isaiah is jumping up and down with his hand raised saying, "Please, please, please pick me. It would be my honor. Whatever You want, it would be my honor!"

You see, my beloved ones, when you get a glimpse of the INFINITE and INTIMATE GOD, everything and everyone else pales.You just want to give Him something, anything,... everything. And in that moment, you realize that He wants... you ... and well... you just exhale!

I almost ended the chapter right there, but I think I will give you a limited view if I don't take this a few steps further, and you will miss the hidden treasures and peace of AWE. You need to know this. GOD answers to no one, and He does not change. He is always TRUE TO HIS CHARACTER. Take a minute and look back over the names and characteristics of GOD that are written in all capital letters in the book so far. Read them slowly. Let their magnitude sink into your being. He is ALWAYS TRUE to these characteristics. And these are just a few of His attributes. Praise God He is the UNWAVERING ONE. This is the key to our peace.

Several years ago, I read two books by Jen Wilken that truly revolutionized my walk with GOD. In the book, *None Like Him*, Jen explores ten ways GOD isn't like us. In the book, *In His Image*, she discusses ten character traits of GOD we should reflect. My appetite was whet to meditate on this MASSIVE GOD Who was nothing like me and yet so loved me. The characteristics mentioned in those books and others revolutionized my walk with MY KING. Calling out His characteristics became the starting point of my prayer life each day. They still are. Today, I called out His characteristics as I began my time with Him. I call them out in praise to GOD, not because He needs to be reminded Who He is, but because I need to be reminded of the character to which He is always true ... I need to be reminded of His ENORMITY THAT DOES NOT CHANGE. For like Isaiah, when I lift my eyes to gaze at Who He is, I am undone... and so are the pulls and chains of this life.

Every day, I praise Him that He is my INCOMPREHENSIBLE, LIMITLESS, ALL POWERFUL, ALL KNOWING, ALWAYS PRESENT, CREATED BY NONE, NEEDING NONE, ETERNAL, UNCHANGING, UNSTOPPABLE, SOVEREIGN [2] .... GOD, KING, REDEEMER, SAVIOR, PARACLETE. I thank Him for being my MOST HOLY, MOST LOVING, MOST GOOD, MOST WISE, MOST GRACIOUS, MOST JUST, MOST MERCIFUL, MOST PATIENT, MOST KIND, MOST TRUE [3] ... FATHER, BRIDEGROOM, SHEPHERD, COMFORTER, TEACHER. Read those slowly. Let the meaning of each soak into your heart. This is our GOD! This is our hope! GOD's undying commitment to His name, His glory, and His character are the very foundation of our hope.

Now let this next point sink into your soul. He alone gets to be GOD, and based on His UNQUESTIONABLE WORTHINESS, this is very, very good news. This point is critical. Our culture's aversion to anything or anyone who is not up for vote or manipulation has left so many holding an illusion of control, crippled by self-will and self choice, and wreaking of entitlement. Sadly, I fear we have allowed the aroma of this to infiltrate the Church, and we have many who are frustrated by or embarrassed by the GOD WHO WILL NOT BE CONTROLLED BY OR MOLDED TO THE CURRENT CULTURE OR TO MY SERVICE. Let this not be true of you, dear ones. You were created ... He redeemed you for so much MORE. Don't let a small, distorted view of the magnitude of GOD or a magnified distorted view of yourself rob you as a believer in CHRIST of the life you were intended to live, the life that is not of this world, the life that is true abundant life... the life of intimacy with GOD ALMIGHTY! Come be amazed with me at the enormity of His character, and join me as we are wonderstruck by the beauty of His ways!!

> **Exodus 15:11-13 says,**
> *"Who is like You among the gods, O Lord? Who is like You, majestic in holiness, awesome in praises, working wonders? You stretched out Your right hand, the earth swallowed them. In Your lovingkindness You have led the people whom You have redeemed; In Your strength You have guided them to Your holy habitation."*

Chapter Three:

Wonderstruck by the Beauty of His Ways (Wowed by how KIND He is)

After a chapter on the enormity of God, perhaps we can fully relate to David's wonder as he declares in **Psalm 8:3-4,** *"When I consider Your heavens, the work of Your fingers, the moon and the stars which You have ordained; what is man that You take thought of him, and the son of man that You care for him?"* When I turn my eyes to the TRUE OMNIPOTENCE and ABSOLUTE MAJESTY of our GOD, I find myself beyond wonderstruck... I find myself at a true loss to try to grasp and explain how or why He would or could be the VERY EMBODIMENT OF LAVISH LOVE.

In the humanness of my mind, I have such difficulty making the two descriptions intertwine. Yet in the chasm of my heart, I so ache for this FULLY KNOWING YET UNCONDITIONALLY LOVING FATHER, this REDEEMER OF ALL THE BROKEN, this AUTHOR OF PEACE, this COMFORTER....this relationship that once and for all seals my significance, chooses my company, and quiets my fears. It seems inside of us there is this missing piece. No matter the award, grade,degree, job, or accolade we receive... no matter the relationship, popularity, gender, marital status, or number of children we attain.... no matter the fault we assign to ourselves or to everyone else... no matter what we do we still hear the echo of that missing piece. Oh beloved ones, we were created for a role dripping with significance.[4] We were created for a relationship beyond all expectations. We were created for a deep, deep peace. The DESIGNER OF OUR FRAME, the SOURCE OF LIFE, the LOVER OF OUR SOULS created us to be whole in the greatest sense of the word. There is a reason for the echo. It goes back to the beginning. Prepare to be wonderstruck.

So much about creation literally bellows the WOW of God. But for now, let's focus on three of His purposes for creating man and ultimately for creating you. The GREAT TRIUNE ORCHESTRATOR OF HEAVEN AND EARTH chooses on day six to make man... in His image. Just let that sink in for a minute. In HIS image. ALMIGHTY GOD creates man to carry His GLORY. Secondly, notice how Adam is assigned to rule over GOD's creation. SOVEREIGN GOD brings the animals to Adam and whatever he names them becomes their name. Don't you love the fatherliness of this picture? Can you fathom this? Man was created to be in a relationship with GOD and in on His plans. Adam and Eve are placed in the most beautiful garden, and every need is met gloriously. They are free to partake without fear, doubt, shame, or lack. OMNISCIENT GOD only withholds one tree... the tree of the knowledge of good and evil. Why would He withhold that one? RELATIONAL GOD offers choice. He has chosen them. Will they choose Him? Eating of this tree would declare, "I will decide for myself what is right and wrong. I will be my own god." Man was created to come under His reign and have no fear. Eating of this tree signified man's rejection of all he had been offered.

Can we just pause a moment and soak on God's original offer in light of His AWESOMENESS? Sometimes I think we say, "God," so flippantly without really grasping His GREATNESS as we refer to Him. Take a minute and just go back over the all capitalized words in the book so far. These are just a shadow of Who He is. Now with that in your mind, take a look at what He offered in the garden. Man was created to carry all that GLORY. Man was created to be in a relationship with and in on the plans of all that MAGNIFICENCE. Man was created to come under the reign of all that LOVING WISDOM and have no fear, no pain, and no shame. As I said before, beloved ones, we were created for a role dripping with significance. We were created for a relationship beyond all expectations. We were created for a deep, deep peace. We were created for so much MORE.

We all know the story. Adam and Eve made their choice. "No thanks, GOD, I will carry my own glory. I will be in a relationship with myself and carry out my own plans. I will decide for myself what is right and wrong." As I have said a million times when talking to children, Adam and Eve stomped their feet and said, "I want to do things my own way. I want to do things my own way. I want to do things... my... own... way." It was the ultimate rebellion. Not to be too blunt, but it was as if they gave GOD the finger and said, "who needs You." Just typing it makes me feel sick to my stomach. It's like I can hear the angels screaming, "What are they doing? NOOOOOO!"

And their spirit died. And every child born after them was born with that same dead spirit... me, you, all of us. The echoing hole was born. The unending and fully unreachable search for significance began. Why would no accomplishment complete the search? When you are built to carry the glory of MASSIVE GOD, no other glory comes close to satisfaction. Why could no relationship satisfy the wound? The intimate relationship with HOLY GOD was severed and shame and selfishness were born. We see it in their first acts as they cover up and blame. Why could nothing silence this deep down dread and anxiety? Fear replaces peace as the footsteps they once eagerly anticipated now lead them to seek cover. Nothing could fill this aching hole their sin had created because it was the size of the GREAT LOVER OF THEIR SOUL, and they had rejected Him.

What would the GOD Who was CREATED BY NONE and NEEDING NONE do? What would ALL POWERFUL GOD choose? Dear one, I will never understand what He chose. I will never be able to fathom or explain why He didn't just wipe out all of humankind and start again. HE CHOSE LOVE. You see LOVE isn't just what GOD does. LOVE is His character and His very essence. LOVE is Who He is! So He did the unthinkable. He came for you. He came for you. He...came... for... you!

JESUS, SON OF GOD, PRINCE OF HEAVEN, WORD OF GOD, LIGHT OF THE WORLD bursts into the darkness in the humblest of ways. GOD HIMSELF becomes one of us to complete the brutally messy work of reconciliation and restoration. The RESCUER, PURCHASER OF RECONCILIATION, and SOURCE OF RESTORATION comes for us! He walks among us, teaches of the Kingdom of GOD, heals, performs miracles, and leads a sinless life. He introduces a radical transition from GOD OF OUR FATHERS to FATHER GOD! COMPASSIONATE JESUS sees us... and grieves with us and for us. INCOMPREHENSIBLE GRACE grieves for the rebels lost in their sin. He grieves! INEXPLICABLE LOVE doesn't shame. He grieves.

> **Matthew 9:36 says,**
> *"Seeing the people, He felt compassion for them, because they were distressed (harassed) and dispirited (thrown down) like sheep without a shepherd."*

The GREAT SHEPHERD saw the invisible ones, grieved, and took action.

Sin must be addressed, and death must be overcome. Enough! So the SON OF THE LIVING GOD because of His INEXPLICABLE LOVE and MATCHLESS GRACE takes on the full wrath of His own violated holiness. Read that sentence again...slowly. All the rebellion, all the audacity of man, all the ensuing pain...fear, anxiety, woundedness, grasping for control, glory robbing, selfishness, sadness, abuse... all of it for all of the ages.... The PERFECT LAMB OF GOD, HIS ONLY SON, GOD HIMSELF willingly takes it all and becomes the WILLING OFFERING FOR THE SINS OF THE WORLD, the WILLING SACRIFICE FOR YOU.

> **John 10:18 says,**
> *"No one has taken it away from Me, but I lay it down on My own initiative. I have authority to lay it down, and I have authority to take it up again. This commandment I received from My Father."*

In the greatest act of SACRIFICIAL LOVE humanity has ever seen, GOD GIVES GOD!! The RIGHTEOUS REDEEMER climbs Calvary's hill, allows the sin of all the ages to be transferred to His account, takes the full and brutal judgment of man's audacious rebellion, experiences the separation, stares into the echoing hole of man's loss, and with LAVISH LOVE and OVERFLOWING GRACE He purchases our freedom with His death. He is buried... staring into the very eyes of death and hell.

Sin must be punished...mission accomplished!

JESUS had said in John 10:10,
"The thief comes only to steal and kill and destroy; I came that they may have life, and have it abundantly."

The GIVER OF ABUNDANT LIFE must deal with death. Hear the drumroll, feel the trembling earth, see the radiant breakthrough in the heavenlies, hear the angelic applause, and sense the relief of the whole earth as the TRUEST LOVE SACRIFICE OF ALL TIME miraculously, through the wonderworking power of OMNIPOTENT GOD, becomes the RESURRECTED GIVER OF ETERNAL LIFE!!!

Death must be defeated and eternal life reinstated... mission accomplished!

And we exhale.... for the first time since the garden.

But the GREAT RESTORER has more for us. He has always

loved closeness, but this time He will move inside of us and transform us from the inside out! We are given the GIFT of the VERY SPIRIT OF GOD living inside of us to be our COMFORTER, TEACHER, GUIDE, HELPER, SHOW-ER OF THINGS TO COME. Try to meditate on that for just a minute not as a mere theological thought but as a relational reality. His SPIRIT in you communing with you and guiding you every moment of every day.

> **Romans 8:15 says,**
> *"For you have not received a spirit of slavery leading to fear again, but you have received a spirit of adoption as sons by which we cry out, 'ABBA! FATHER!'"*

Purpose must be restored ... mission accomplished!

Now this part is critical. Don't miss this most important point, my dear ones. I am about to share with you the difference between knowing about JESUS and really knowing JESUS. I fear so many really good church members know about Him but have missed true salvation and new life. JESUS is LOVE THAT DEMANDS A RESPONSE... and the response is ALL. As the old hymn says, "LOVE SO AMAZING, LOVE SO DIVINE demands my soul, my life, my all."[5] For just as in the garden Adam and Eve had to choose, we must choose to accept the LOVE GIFT OF ETERNAL LIFE. He offers TRUE LOVE AND ABUNDANT LIFE, and we must accept HIs offer. He offers the ALL of Himself, and He wants the same in return. I want to be fully honest here. This isn't a partnership. This is a full surrender. It costs

... everything... nothing held back...your life and your all. It requires repentance and returning.

> **Acts 3:19 says,**
> *"Therefore repent and return, so that your sins may be wiped away, in order that times of refreshing may come from the presence of the LORD."*

Oh my precious one, this is what I so desperately want for each of you... times of refreshing from the presence of the LORD! Quite honestly, it is the heartbeat of this book... refreshing peace and intimacy with the GOD WHO IS SO VERY REAL! But for this to be yours, you must be His. You must personally repent and return.

Repentance is almost a dirty word in our society, yet that is the stated cost. What is repentance? I love this definition.. "The doctrine of repentance as taught in the Bible is a call to persons to make a radical turn from one way of life to another. The repentance (metanoia) called for throughout the Bible is a summons to a personal, absolute and ultimate unconditional surrender to God as Sovereign. Though it includes sorrow and regret, it is more than that. It is a call to conversion from self-love, self-trust, and self-assertion to obedient trust and self-commitment to now live for God and his purposes."[6]

As I have always told children, accepting JESUS is saying, "Good-bye, my way. Hello, GOD's way." My precious one, let me say this as gently as I can. The cost is ...your everything... which quite honestly without Him is nothing but that echoing hole that cannot be filled no matter what you do, who you become, or where you go. Make no mistake, He requires a full trade. All of Him for all of you. Many may have misled you to believe you just say a few words, go to church, and live your life as you choose. That isn't the TRUE GOSPEL. Your glory, your plans, and your self rule are completely traded for the glory, the plans, and the reign of the LOVER OF YOUR SOUL, SOURCE OF ALL WISDOM, and RIGHTFUL KING OF YOUR LIFE. Praise GOD, He doesn't leave us as a cleaned up version of ourselves. That wouldn't be true to His TRUE LOVE. He completely transforms us!

Repent and return... to where do you return? He has offered us a return to Eden. Eden. The very name means delight. Delight was the original intention. Man would delight in GOD and GOD would hold man. Delight...relationship... glory ... peace... significance. Do you remember those three purposes for which man was created in the beginning? Man would carry the glory of GOD, he would be in a relationship with GOD and participate in His plans, and he would come under His reign and have no fear. The ALL-ENCOMPASSING GRACIOUS RESCUING LOVE of our BELOVED REDEEMER GOD says we can return right there! We trade our 90 seconds on earth of trying to twist ourselves and everyone else to fill a gaping hole for ... an eternity in relationship with the GOD OF THE UNIVERSE and in love with the DEFINITION OF LOVE ITSELF. We trade the echoing hole of striving for the REVERBERATING WHOLENESS of our BELOVED JESUS.

Life, relationship, purpose, peace, freedom... oh my beloved ones, don't you see? SAVIOR JESUS purchased all of those back for us! JUSTICE has been served, MERCY has been given, and GRACE has been offered. LOVE wins! LOVE wins! LOVE wins!

SUCH TREMENDOUS GRACE calls us to happily forsake and surrender all. SUCH AMAZING LOVE leaves us speechless and leads us right back to the peace of His reign and the safety of His heart! Oh how He loves you!! Won't you join me in being ...Wonderstruck by the Beauty of His Ways that **"the times of refreshing may come from the presence of the LORD!!"**

John 3:16 –
"For GOD so loved the world, that He gave His ONLY BEGOTTEN SON, that whoever believes in Him shall not perish, but have eternal life."

Chapter Four:

More Wonderstruck by the Beauty of His Ways (Wowed by how KIND He is)

Part Two (because there is MORE)

"Could we with ink the ocean fill,
And were the skies of parchment made,
Were every stalk on earth a quill,
And every man a scribe by trade;
To write the love of God above
Would drain the ocean dry;
Nor could the scroll contain the whole,
Though stretched from sky to sky." [7]

These words from the hymn, *"The Love of God,"* paint one of the most beautiful word pictures I know of the indescribable expanse of the LOVE of God. They also quell the sequential voice in my head that is telling me to move on to the E of AWE. If the whole of the universe can't contain the words, surely I can dedicate another chapter to encouraging my beloved ones to wade even deeper into MATCHLESS LOVE. Surely we can pause a moment and soak in the INDESCRIBABLE marriage of the AWESOMENESS of GOD and the WONDROUS LOVE of GOD.

One beautiful aspect of the character of GOD is His IMMUTABILITY... the fact that He is CHANGELESS. He is ABSOLUTE. He cannot change. One reason this matters, dear ones, is that GOD doesn't take off one part of His character to put on another one. In other words, He doesn't take off His HOLINESS to be LOVING. He is HOLY LOVE and LOVINGLY HOLY. He doesn't surrender His OMNIPOTENCE to be INTIMATE. He is ALL POWERFUL INTIMACY. So along this vein, understand that He is LIMITLESS LOVE, ALWAYS PRESENT LOVE, ALL KNOWING LOVE, ETERNAL LOVE, UNSTOPPABLE LOVE, JUST LOVE....well you get the picture.

Do you remember earlier in the book where I mentioned my grief that perhaps my generation had misrepresented GOD to you in our desire to be sure you didn't miss grace? Here is the point of that grief. To speak of the LOVE of GOD outside of His AWESOMENESS cheapens His WONDER and leaves us open to entitlement and a me-centered gospel. Carrying this emotion-based definition of love, many find themselves frustrated, bitter, and walking away from a TRUE LOVE that won't be puppeted by their will or surrender to their limited view of what is best. DIVINE LOVE surpasses emotion, though the emotion is beyond deep as it touches the very depth of my aching hole and brings wholeness. HOLY LOVE is TENACIOUS FOR MY ULTIMATE AND ETERNAL GOOD. RIGHTEOUS LOVE sets everything right... and finally I can exhale.

Perhaps our issue is with the definition of love... real love... the kind GOD has for His people. Perhaps we can't fathom SACRIFICIAL LOVE that transforms us from rebels completely alienated and dead in our sin to children who are beloved and chosen. Can we step back from our cultural lens of the meaning of love for a minute and see how GOD defines love? I believe you will see with me LOVE SO POWERFUL it defies explanation.

Song of Solomon 8:6-7 says,
"Put me like a seal over your heart, like a seal on your arm. For love is as strong as death, jealousy is as severe as Sheol; Its flashes are flashes of fire, the very flame of the LORD. Many waters cannot quench love, nor will rivers overflow it; If a man were to give all the riches of his house for love, it would be utterly despised."

God is LOVE. LOVE is His very essence. Based on this passage alone, He is...

FULLY COMMITTED NEVER WAVERING LOVE
LOVE AS STRONG AS DEATH
UNDYING LOVE
LOVE THAT TENACIOUSLY CALLS TO FULL ABANDONMENT
ALL CONSUMING PASSIONATE LOVE
INEXTINGUISHABLE LOVE EVEN IF TROUBLES ARISE
FAITHFUL LOVE EVEN IF SITUATIONS INTENSIFY
LOVE THAT CAN'T BE SWEPT AWAY BY SEASONS OR
CULTURAL CHANGES
BEYOND PRICE OR IMAGINATION LOVE
LOVE WORTHY OF MY ALL

This is how He loves you... with all His heart!!

1 Corinthians 13 says,

"If I speak with the tongues of men and of angels, but do not have love, I have become a noisy gong or a clanging cymbal. If I have the gift of prophecy and know all mysteries and all knowledge, and if I have all faith so as to remove mountains, but do not have love, I am nothing. And if I give all my possessions to feed the poor, and if I surrender my body to be burned, but do not have love, it profits me nothing.
Love is patient, love is kind and is not jealous; love does not brag and is not arrogant, does not act unbecomingly; it does not seek its own; is not provoked, does not take into account a wrong suffered, does not rejoice in unrighteousness, but rejoices with the truth; bears all things, believes all things, hopes all things, endures all things.

Love never fails; but if there are gifts of prophecy, they will be done away; if there are tongues, they will cease; if there is knowledge, it will be done away. For we know in part and we prophesy in part; but when the perfect comes, the partial will be done away. When I was a child, I used to speak like a child, think like a child, reason like a child; when I became a man, I did away with childish things. For now we see in a mirror dimly, but then face to face; now I know in part, but then I will know fully just as I also have been fully known. But now faith, hope, love, abide these three; but the greatest of these is love."

Again, GOD is LOVE. LOVE is His very essence. Based on this passage, He is LOVE that is...

PATIENT, KIND, WAITING and CALLING, GENTLE,

DESIRING OUR BEST, FAITHFUL, SACRIFICIAL, FOR US, APPROACHABLE, FORGIVING, HOPEFUL and REASSURING, EXCITED WHEN WE SEE THE TRUTH, PROTECTING HURTING PLACES, ALWAYS BELIEVING THE BEST, ALWAYS HOPEFUL, ENDURING, NEVER FAILING, and THE GREATEST GIFT.

Take a moment and read back over all the descriptors in all capital letters (in the whole book if you have a few moments). Those aren't fleeting descriptors, they are His very nature and the essence of His LOVE for you. This is no weak willed, leave you like you are even if it hurts you kind of love. This is HURRICANE FORCE LOVE.... truly encountering it leaves you ... wrecked.

To catch a glimpse of the AWESOMENESS of GOD and then realize the TRUE LOVE of GOD leads to a GOD-centered gospel where I want to give Him absolutely everything. I find myself filled with wonderstruck adoration and worship, and l hunger for more of Him. The disciples were so undone by His LOVE, they left all to follow and were willing to face loss, imprisonment, beatings, and even death. What caused that kind of loyalty? They were just wrecked by LOVE.

John is my favorite disciple. Who couldn't love a guy who called himself "the disciple whom JESUS loved"? Quite honestly, he didn't start with that dedication. His early encounters with the MASTER resound with "What's in it for me?" So what changed him? I did a study once trying to look at John's encounters with JESUS through his eyes. I just don't think John could get over the fact that GOD'S SON was here, and He was UNMATCHABLE STRENGTH and HUMBLE LOVE. When John saw the cost, when he saw the plan of salvation, when he looked back over all the LORD had said... I think he was just undone. You can hear His amazement throughout the book of 1 John.

1 John 3:1-

"See how great a love the Father has bestowed on us, that we would be called children of God; and such we are. For this reason the world does not know us because it did not know Him."

1 John 4:10-

"In this is love, not that we loved God but that He loved us and sent His Son to be the propitiation for our sins."

1 John 4:16-

"We have come to know and have believed the love which God has for us. God is love and the one who abides in love abides in God and God abides in him."

I love these passages because it is like John is almost giddy saying, "Can you believe it? GOD loves us!!! I mean He really loves us! Wait, did you hear me? We witnessed it. It is true. GOD loves us!!!!." Church history tells us they boiled John in oil. He was exiled to Patmos. Nothing would shake him. Why? He had encountered GOD INCARNATE and He was REAL LOVE.

John was not the only one. Take a look at Paul...religious expert, Pharisee, Hebrew of the Hebrews, following all the rules, sure he was righteous, zealous to the point of killing people who disagreed... Paul. Paul encounters GLORIOUS JESUS on the road to Damascus and his life is fully flipped. Paul's life basically says, "Here is my resume, here are my opinions, here is my pedigree, here is my self-righteousness, here are my plans, give me a new friend group, send me to prison, whatever you need to do... just give me JESUS." What could cause such reckless abandon? Hear it from Paul himself. Who did Paul find JESUS to be?

> Romans 5:8-
> *"But God demonstrates His own love toward us in that while we were yet sinners, Christ died for us."*
> (UNCONDITIONAL DEMONSTRATIVE LOVE NOT DEPENDENT ON ME
>
> Romans 8:31-
> *"What then shall we say to these things? If God is for us, who is against us?"*
> (LOVE THAT IS FOR US)
>
> Romans 8:35-
> *"Who will separate us from the love of Christ? Will tribulation, or distress, or persecution, or famine, or nakedness, or peril, or sword?"*
> (LOVE BEYOND ANY SEPARATION)
>
> Romans 8:37-
> *"But in all these things, we overwhelmingly conquer through Him Who loved us."*
> (VICTORIOUS LOVE)
>
> Romans 8:38-39-
> *"For I am convinced that neither death, nor life, nor angels, nor principalities, nor things present, nor things to come, nor powers, nor height, nor depth, nor any other created thing, will*

be able to separate us from the love of God,
Jesus our Lord."
(LOVE BIGGER THAN DEATH OR LIFE
LOVE LOUDER THAN ANGELS OR DEMON$
LOVE STRONGER THAN WHAT I SEE
LOVE STRONGER THAN WHAT IS COMING
LOVE MORE POWERFUL THAN POWER STRUGGLES
LOVE GREATER THAN MY HIGHEST HIGH
LOVE DEEPER THAN MY DEEPEST LOW
LOVE SURER THAN THE OPINIONS OF MAN
IMMOVABLE LOVE)

Paul was Amazed by the enormity of His character...
Paul was Wonderstruck by the beauty of His ways...
Paul was Enraptured by the reality of His presence...

Paul fell in AWE. He would never be the same.

And when we catch a true glimpse of the AWESOMENESS OF GOD and the MATCHLESS TENACIOUS LOVE OF GOD...neither will we.

Philippians 3:7-8
"But whatever things were gain to me, those things I have
counted as loss for the sake of Christ. More than that, I count
all things to be loss in view of the surpassing value of knowing
Christ Jesus my Lord, for Whom I have suffered the loss of all
things, and count them but rubbish so that I may gain Christ."

Chapter Five:

Enraptured by the Reality of His Presence
(Excited by how REAL and PRESENT He is)

I come to the garden alone,
While the dew is still on the roses,
And the voice I hear falling on my ear
The Son of God discloses.

And He walks with me, and He talks with me,
And He tells me I am His own;
And the joy we share as we tarry there,
None other has ever known. [8]

Beloved ones, I almost feel I should ask you to reverently remove your shoes as we enter this next chapter.... and at the same time I feel almost jump-up-and-down giddy with the excitement of introducing you to the most intimate and transforming opportunity you will ever experience. Perhaps this inexplicable mixture of speechless worship and uncontainable joy and "at homeness" is a good word picture for being enraptured by the reality of His Presence. As the song

above explains... the ALMIGHTY GOD OF THE UNIVERSE, LOVE
PERSONIFIED, the GREAT I AM, the KING OF KINGS AND LORD
OF LORDS, THE LOVER OF MY SOUL, the ONE WHO KNOWS
MY FRAME AND ITS WEAKNESS, the GOD WHO SEES ALL, the
ONE WHO CALLS EARTH HIS FOOTSTOOL.... "HE walks with
me, and HE talks with me,and HE tells me I am His own." Every
day. In any given moment. In every season of life. Every time
my eyes turn to Him. Each time my heart or my words cry out.
Oh my dear ones, can I proclaim with all I am that HE is REAL,
HE is WORTHY, HE is WORTH ALL, HE is the TRANSFORMING
TREASURE, and HE wants to be with you.

I must say I am truly mystified by the relational nature
of GOD. Why? Why does HE desire closeness with us? Yet
throughout Scripture, His desire for relationship with a
people He would call His own and His desire to be near is a
constant theme. As Ann VosKamp describes in *The Greatest
Gift: Unwrapping the Full Love Story of Christmas*, we find Him
walking in the garden looking for Adam and Eve. We see Him
in the cloud by day and the fire by night with the children of
Israel. We note Him meeting Moses in the tent of meeting and
carefully designing a portable tabernacle so He could travel with
His people in the wilderness. We find Him in the Holy of Holies
behind the veil of the temple in Jerusalem.[9] We find HIM... the
RELENTLESS PURSUER, the LONG-SUFFERING KEEPER OF
COVENANT, the ALWAYS FAITHFUL GOD... calling His people to
return His faithfulness and draw near. Note the themes...WITH...
NEAR.

Then in the most baffling display of RELATIONAL LOVE and
INCONCEIVABLE GRACE, GOD takes "withness" to a whole new

level. EMMANUEL, GOD WITH US, the WORD OF GOD, the SON OF GOD HIMSELF, KING JESUS bursts quietly and supernaturally on the scene. HE comes to be with us. HE comes to bring us back to HIMSELF. And the life JESUS lives here... the life which **Hebrews 1:3 says is the "radiance of God's glory and the exact representation of His nature"**... screams personal relationship and closeness. JESUS was daily with HIS people... seeing them (especially when they felt invisible), teaching them, correcting them, healing them, warning them, showing them what was to come, protecting them, loving them, empowering them, revealing His plans and His amazing glory to them... flipping their lives and transforming them!

But there is MORE. In the final hours of His earthly life... knowing the agony of the cross is just hours away... JESUS raises the bar of intimacy beyond human comprehension with this promise,,,

> **John 16:7,**
> *"But I tell you the truth, it is to your advantage that I go away; for if I do not go away, the Helper will not come to you; but if I go, I will send Him to you."*

He goes on to explain that this HELPER is the very SPIRIT OF GOD, and HE is moving inside of them (talk about relational nearness and withness)!! To really grasp the significance of this...

> **1 Corinthians 2:11-12 says,**
> *"For who among men knows the thoughts of a man except the*

spirit of the man which is in him? Even so the thoughts of God no one knows except the Spirit of God. Now we have received, not the spirit of the world, but the Spirit who is from God, so that we may know the things freely given to us by God."

The VERY ESSENCE OF GOD, the ONE WHO KNOWS THE THOUGHTS OF GOD would live inside of us. He would be our PARACLETE- ONE CALLED BESIDE, COMFORTER, GUIDE, TEACHER, ANOINTER, SEAL, GUARD, HELPER, and EQUIPPER. In John 16, JESUS promised the SPIRIT OF TRUTH would guide us into all the truth, disclose what is to come, glorify JESUS and further disclose His ways to us. He would speak to us, and we would obey. He would empower us, and we would fulfill our purpose. He would show us the glory of GOD, and we would abound in AWE. Do you see it?? We would carry His glory, be in relationship with Him and in on His plans, and come under His reign and have no fear... not just in heaven...but here...every day... every moment... in intimate communion.

Following the promise of the Holy Spirit and just moments before the betrayal and crucifixion, JESUS displays His UNWAVERING DEVOTION to His people in John 17 when He prays for those He loves. He prays for us. Just soak that in a moment. JESUS is SOVEREIGN and OMNISCIENT. He knew what was coming on the cross. He knew the rejection, punishment, shame, and pain He had to carry if He was to be our RECONCILER and return us to GOD. So what did He do in those final moments? He prayed for His dear companions... He prayed for us. Our RELATIONAL MASTER, the EXACT REPRESENTATION OF HIS NATURE, the RADIANCE OF HIS GLORY said...

John 17:3,
"This is eternal life, that they may know You, the only true God, and Jesus Christ whom You have sent."

The LIFE He was about to die to secure was all about the GOD YOU CAN KNOW. The very essence of ABUNDANT LIFE He spoke of in John 10 was the knowing. Knowing...really knowing... and communing... and being with ... enraptured by ... the reality of His Presence. Every day. All day. Every season. Each moment. Wow!

The CHAMPION OF OUR CLOSENESS goes on to pray for some specific things we will need here... before heaven. You see, salvation isn't just about experiencing His Presence in heaven one day. Though heaven will be amazing, JESUS didn't say eternal life was heaven. He said eternal life was **"knowing YOU, the ONLY TRUE GOD, and JESUS CHRIST WHOM YOU SENT."** Real life is really knowing Him! Our LOVING ADVOCATE asked His FATHER for the following for us ... for our time here...for the knowing...

John 17:11-
"Keep them in Your Name."

John 17:15-
"Keep them from the evil one."

John 17:17-
"Sanctify them (set them apart) in the truth."

John 17:21-
"That they may all be one, even as You, Father, are in Me and

*I in You, that they also may be in Us, so that the world may
believe that you sent me."*

John 17:24-
"Be with Me where I am so they can see My glory."

John 17:26-
*"The love with which You loved Me may be in them, and I in
them."*

Do you hear His plea for His beloved ones? Guard them,
protect them, set them apart in truth, unify them, show them
My glory, fill them with the love You have for Me... let them join
Us. The prayer calls for us to be pulled in close so we can know
Him. Moments later He would take on the agony of the cross to
make that possible. Moments later He would breathe His last,
and the veil between us and the HOLY OF HOLIES would be torn
inviting us to come know. Three days later, He would defeat
death once and for all becoming our RESURRECTED SAVIOR and
PURCHASER OF ETERNAL LIFE.... that life where we know Him...
really know Him... and draw near.

1 Peter 3:18-
*"For Christ also died for sins once for all, the just for the unjust,
so that He might <u>bring us to God</u>, having been put to death in
the flesh, but made alive in the Spirit."*

Hebrews 10:19-22-
*"Therefore, brethren, since we have confidence to enter the
holy place by the blood of Jesus, by a new and living way which*

*He inaugurated for us through the veil, that is, His flesh, and
since we have a great priest over the house of God, let us <u>draw
near with a sincere heart</u> in full assurance of faith, having our
hearts sprinkled clean from an evil conscience and our bodies
washed with pure water."*

Do you see it, dear ones? ALWAYS FAITHFUL GOD literally
moved heaven and earth and overcame sin and death to bring
you to Himself... not just at the end of your life or at the end of
the age, but today... right now... in this moment. The saddest
possibility on earth would be if you never received His gift of
life for yourself and missed salvation... missed Him. The next
saddest possibility on earth would be if you received SALVATION
FOR ETERNITY and missed GLORIOUS INTIMACY FOR TODAY.

Our life on earth is really just the dress rehearsal for
eternity. What will eternity be like for those who are His?...
constantly beholding His breath-taking glory, awe-struck in
praise and adoration, finally at peace under His omniscient and
loving reign, joyfully following His always good commands, face
to face withness with MAJESTY and LOVE ITSELF...complete
contentment...HOME. If my life here on earth is the dress
rehearsal for this reality, wouldn't my daily practice be to turn
my eyes toward recognizing His GLORY? Wouldn't praise and
adoration constantly flow from my lips and my life? Wouldn't
surrender and obedience not be subject to the whims of my own
feelings, but instead be my one assurance of peace? Wouldn't
coming away with Him in this divine preview of the glory of
heaven... wouldn't HE... become MY ONE TRUE OBSESSION?

INCOMPREHENSIBLE HOLINESS and LIMITLESS LOVE

moved heaven and earth to be with me. OMNISCIENT MERCY and EVER PRESENT GRACE literally gave His life to draw me near. IMMUTABLE KINDNESS, UNSTOPPABLE WISDOM, AND SOVEREIGN GOODNESS actually moved inside of me to show me how REAL and PRESENT He is. Could I have any other response than to joyfully and so very gratefully draw near?

And when I draw near... when I come heavy with the cares of this life... when I come scared and unsure of what to do... on the many days fear has made me barely able to crawl to the secret place with Him... when my inadequacies are screaming and the responsibilities are mounting... when I am alone or the days I am weary from the people...when I feel invisible or unimportant... when my pain seems unnoticed and my needs seem impossible to meet...when I don't know how to be a good wife, mother, daughter, and friend... and I draw near and just say, "FATHER." I can't explain it, but in that one word call.... HE comes... GOD gives GOD... HIS TRANSFORMING PRESENCE stills my racing mind and calms my shaking heart and I exhale. "And He walks with me and He talks with me. And He tells me I am His own. And the joy we share as we tarry there, none other has ever known." There is knowing for today. There is closeness for today. There is HIM for today. He is REAL and HE is PRESENT. Draw near.

Psalm 116:1-2-
"I love the LORD, because He hears my voice and my supplications. Because He has inclined His ear to me, therefore I shall call upon Him as long as I live."

SECTION TWO:

Drawing Near: A Love Story

Psalm 34:4-5-

"_I sought the LORD, and He answered me_, and delivered me from all my fears. They looked to Him and were radiant, and their faces will never be ashamed."

Chapter Six:

A Cry for Intimacy

Our God is a DIVINE STORYTELLER, and love stories are His specialty. These are no light-hearted romantic comedies He writes. No, He is the AUTHOR of transformational love stories, the kind of stories that leave the characters amazed, wonderstruck, and enraptured (in AWE) and quite honestly aching for MORE. I know because I have been living in one of His love stories for over fifty years, and I feel I have only scratched the surface of its depth. There is a wall hanging I often see in home decor stores that says, "Every love story is beautiful, but ours is my favorite." I have to be honest and say that although some of the plot lines scare me at first, I trust the love story the GREAT ARTIST is painting with my life. He is the MASTER CHOREOGRAPHER OF STEPS, and I would like to share a little bit of our transforming dance with you. My goal, dear ones, is not in any way to give you a template for your own story. GOD's way of loving His own cannot be reduced to a formula. My goal in sharing our love story is to awaken in you an awareness of the very personal love story He wants to write with you and to spark in you a desire to embrace it fully and declare it yours.

As we saw in the last chapter, our AWE INSPIRING GOD is RELATIONAL and INTIMATE. He desires closeness with those He loves, His people. He died to make it possible. Because we were created by Him in His image for the purpose of a relationship with Him, we find ourselves craving His IMMENSENESS and His INTIMACY. Yet from our human standpoint, it is difficult for our finite minds to bring those two characteristics into balance. I heard a message by Miles FIddell of Auburn Community Church that explained it this way. "Our chief ambition is to know the heart of GOD. It is impossible to know His heart without reverent fear AND relational friendship. We must have the combination to trust the heart of GOD."[10]

Herein lies the challenge. Quite honestly, this challenge is one of the main reasons I am writing this book for you, my precious ones. Satan does not want us to know the SOVEREIGN **and** MAGNANIMOUS heart of God fully. He knows that such a love affair is transformational and freeing for us and dangerous for him. The enemy works very hard to keep us totally away from GOD, but if he is unsuccessful in that move, his next strategy is to have us focus only on one facet of GOD's nature to the exclusion of the other. The result of his singularly focused ploy is some Christians walking in such fear, they never draw near to the heart of GOD, and some Christians treating GOD with such flippant familiarity that they totally miss His GREATNESS. Either choice leaves us lacking, craving, and often scrambling for something MORE.

Psalm 25:14 -

"The secret (intimacy) of the LORD is for those who fear Him, and He will make them know His covenant."

It was that craving that led me to ask the LORD for something very specific. When I tell our love story (after salvation of course), I have to start with that request. But first, let me give you a little background.

You see dear ones, I accepted JESUS as my SAVIOR when I was just a child of around six years old. I was blessed to grow up in a Christian home and went to a very conservative Christian school. I feared the LORD and was quite aware of His HOLINESS. For that reason, I tried very hard to please Him in all the ways I thought honored His requirements... going to church, following the do's and don'ts, and trying very hard to be perfect. As a perfectionist by nature, I was a pretty good performer. Legalism paired with a type A personality makes for quite a task master, and I worked hard to follow the rules even though the performance was sometimes paralyzing. Please don't misunderstand. I was His. I worshipped Him. I loved Him. I tried to honor and obey Him. I had known HIM as my SAVIOR and MASTER for quite some time, but I saw something in a friend that made me want MORE.

My friend, Lynn, loved to talk about her FRIEND, JESUS. The relationship she described with Him was one of laughter, sharing, understanding, love, and joy. I knew she was His. Like me, she worshipped Him. She loved Him. She tried to honor and obey Him. But she also seemed to enjoy Him. I felt I was missing something I craved. Lynn and I had many conversations with me sharing His HOLINESS and her sharing His GRACE. She will tell you today that GOD used those conversations to plant seeds that led her to His AWESOMENESS, and I can tell you that GOD used those conversations to lead me to crave His LOVE. (As a side note, do you see what an INCREDIBLE DIRECTOR OF STEPS He is? He led us to each other, so neither one of us would miss ALL of Him. WOW!) So I decided to ask.

As best as I can remember, the prayer went something like this, "LORD, I love You and I obey You, but I wish I was in love with You." I believe that prayer pleased Him. I wonder if He had been waiting for me to notice that He desired that, too. My life was changed by that request, and I wonder if something shifted in the heavenlies. All I know is that He began to orchestrate events in my life as only He can to begin our walk of intimacy... to answer that prayer. He didn't zap me with feelings of love. It doesn't work that way. At least it didn't for me. No, He began to woo my heart. Several decades later, He is still wooing. Tears fill my eyes as I write this. I am still undone by His AMAZING LOVE. GOD HIMSELF sees me and knows me and woos me to His MATCHLESS HEART. If you are His and you still yourself for a minute, you will hear Him wooing you, too.

A few weeks after this prayer, I was asked to speak at a women's retreat for our church. I happily agreed and asked what they wanted me to share. The retreat was about self-esteem. Now, my beloved ones, I am going to get very real with you right now and show you behind my curtain. I am not proud of what you are about to see, but you need to see it to understand our love story. So I agreed to the topic, but the conversation in my head went something like this, "Ugh. Why do women always want to whine about their self-esteem? I don't really struggle with this, but ok." Looking back, I wince at that internal conversation. How could I have been so clueless? I wonder if the LOVER OF MY SOUL and KNOWER OF MY FRAME shook His head a little and smiled knowing what He had in store for me. Anyway, I approached our pastor for suggested reading material. He gave me several books, and among them was the book, *The Search for Significance*[11]. I began reading. The wooing was underway.

I think *The Search for Significance* is a must read for every believer. I won't share all the details, but the book describes (and nullifies with truth) the lies we believe in our quest for the personal significance He designed us to get from Him alone. Needless to say, I realized my "lack of issue with significance" was a scam, and I was made acutely aware that my quest for significance had not only put me in bondage but had distorted my view of GOD's ENORMOUS GRACE. So much is to be gained from the study, but here is the life changing point the WRITER OF OUR LOVE STORY most had for me..."I am deeply loved by GOD. There is nothing I can do to make Him love me more and nothing I can do to make Him love me less. His love for me is perfect, so I don't have to be afraid." I know that sounds simple, but for me it was a true GRACE awakening.

> **1 John 4:18-19 -**
> *"There is no fear in love; but perfect (complete) love casts out fear, because fear involves punishment (torment), and the one who fears is not perfected in love. We love because He first loved us."*

I knew about the GRACE that gave us salvation, but I have to honestly say I don't think I had any concept of DAILY GRACE. I knew He loved the world, but somehow I had the notion that His PERSONAL LOVE for me was somehow tied to my performance and whether I got it just right. I thought following all the rules made me confident, but it really made me enslaved and fearful. I had told GOD I wanted to be "in love" with Him... so... He wowed me with how much He loved me!! THE ALL KNOWING ONE loved me. THE HOLY ONE loved me. THE GREAT I AM loved me. HE... loved...me!!! I was significant to GOD simply because He was PERFECT LOVE, and He chose me! His love for me had nothing to do with me and everything to do with His PURSUING HEART. The wooing of the ALMIGHTY had begun.

I was chosen, not because of anything I had done but simply because the RANSOMING PRINCE had set His heart on me! MATCHLESS LOVE had more to show me. I wanted to be in love with Him. He knew that began with opening my eyes to His OVERFLOWING LOVE for me.

Ephesians 1: 3 says,
"Blessed be the God and Father of our Lord Jesus Christ, who has blessed us with every spiritual blessing in the heavenly places in Christ."

The rest of Ephesians chapter one is like an open vat of His love that gushes out declaring who I am simply because I am His. In CHRIST, I am...Blessed, Chosen, Holy, Blameless, Loved, Predestined, Adopted, Grace- bestowed, Beloved, Redeemed, Forgiven , Grace-lavished, Knower of the mystery (all things in

Christ), Having obtained an inheritance, Sealed in Him with the Holy Spirit of promise, Having His pledge.

I...am...His...and...I ...am... loved...and that changes everything.

How had I missed it? He had been showing His UNCONDITIONAL LOVE all along. I had been so busy trying to please Him, I hadn't noticed He was already pleased...not because of my performance but because of HIS. I am completely loved because of His character (LOVE) and my position (His)!

I also hadn't noticed He was sending me, "I love yous," every single day. So the STORYTELLER provided another chapter for our love story. About seven years ago, He made sure Ann Voskamp's book, *One Thousand Gifts*[12], landed in my hands. While sitting on the beach soaking in the enormity of the CREATOR, He gently challenged me to open my eyes to those love gifts the GIVER OF ALL GOOD THINGS was sending me every day and encouraged me to write them down. Could I write down those things that brought me joy...the deep and the seemingly frivolous... and realize every single one of them was from Him? So I accepted the challenge and started a list. Had all of those blessings been there all along? Were they valentines from MY BELOVED that I never opened? Could He really be declaring His CONSTANT LOVE.... constantly? Seven years later, I have listed over ten thousand love gifts from OUR GREAT GOD. Those are just the ones I remembered to write down. Remember those valentine boxes we made as children to hold our valentines? Look... really look... inside the valentine box of your everyday life and see what He may be putting unnoticed in your box.

Valentine's Day is every day with the CONSUMING FLAME OF LOVE.

I asked to fall in love with GOD.

He showed me how much HE loved me.

And the embers of my heart began to burn.

Little did I know, He was just getting started. A WILDFIRE OF LOVE was coming!

Chapter Seven:

The Living Love Letter...
Love Has a Name

" For a day in Your courts is better than a thousand outside.
I would rather stand at the threshold of the house of my God
than dwell in the tents of wickedness. For the LORD God is a sun and
shield; The LORD gives grace and glory; No good thing
does He withhold from those who walk uprightly.
O LORD of hosts, how blessed is the man who trusts in You!."
Psalm 84:10-12

Beloved ones, at this point I so wish I could sit across the table from you, and look deeply into your eyes and somehow put into words the ENORMOUS LOVE of our GRACIOUS AND GLORIOUS GOD. The amazing thing about GOD's love is that if you truly experience it, you may find it difficult for it not to become your MAGNIFICENT OBSESSION. As I told you in the last chapter, I had asked to fall in love with GOD. He began by showing me His MATCHLESS GRACE... how much He loved me. But that was just the beginning. I had another prayer request for the BLAZING FLAME OF LOVE, and He had more to show me than I had dared dream.

Many years ago, I remember reading or hearing about a great father of the faith who had an experience with the love of GOD. The way I remember the description was that he described it as, "wave after wave of His love came over me such that I thought I would die if He did not stop." I also have a dear friend who said that one time he went to the pulpit to speak and the LORD OF LOVE allowed him to experience His love for the people in the room. My friend said all he could do was stand there and weep. I wanted that very real experience with the love of GOD. So I asked! For many years, I asked something like this, "Lord, I would like to experience that wave after wave of Your love such that I feel I will die if you don't stop." I prayed this often and looked forward to the day I would have my prayer answered. As a side note, if you haven't known the WRITER OF THE POETIC STORY very long, can I tell you that He often answers prayers in a way nothing like what you thought. His story is always so much better, but if you aren't careful, you might miss the ORCHESTRATOR OF SYMPHONY because you are listening for your favorite jingle.

I realized just a few months ago that the DESIRE OF MY HEART had answered both my prayers..... the one to be in love with Him and the one to experience His love...in a way not like anything I had ever expected. As always, the ANSWERER OF HEART PRAYERS had answered so much better and given so much more fully than I had envisioned in my plan of how He would do what I asked. Let me take you behind the scenes of the last decade or more as the CONSUMING FIRE WHO CALLS ME

TO COME CLOSE threw open the doors of GRACE and GLORY and invited me inside.

> **John 17:25-26 says,**
> *"O righteous Father, although the world has not known You, yet I have known You; and these have known that You sent Me;* <u>*and I have made Your name known to them, and will make it known, so that the love with which You loved Me may be in them, and I in them."*</u>

JESUS is completing His beautiful prayer for His disciples right before purchasing our salvation on the cross. There is a nugget of truth in the last line of that prayer that has proven to be the LIFELINE OF LOVE that my BELOVED has used to truly give me the answer to my prayers for intimacy. The secret to experiencing His love is... knowing His Name.

Do you remember the story of when GOD showed His glory to Elijah? Do you remember how GOD wasn't in the great wind or the earthquake or the fire, but He was in the gentle breeze? Discovering the secret to His love for me was like that breeze... like a secret love note sent under a desk... I didn't even realize what He was doing at first. He was giving me MORE THAN I ASKED FOR ... GOD was giving GOD!

The GREAT ADVENTURE started so unobtrusively. We were on a family vacation (at the beach, of course). Among the books I had packed for beach reading was a little booklet by Beth Moore called, *Discovering God's Purpose for Your Life*[13]. The book was based on the following verse:

Philippians 3:10 [Amplified Bible]–
"My determined purpose is to know Him, progressing in intimacy, that I may perceive and recognize and understand the wonders of His being."

Somehow through that little booklet, GOD whispered the idea that if we were going to grow closer, I had to know HIM. I wrote at the top of a piece of paper, "Who is My God?" Underneath that title, I wrote the verse above. I casually started a list of names and characteristics He revealed to me in my day to day walk with Him. Sometimes it was through a sermon or Bible study. Sometimes it was through a song. Sometimes it was through something someone said. Sometimes it was through a crisis. I just would notice this quiet little nudge (GENTLE BREEZE) like He was saying, "Did you catch Who that says I am?" I would write it down on the dog-eared little list in my Bible. The first ten...

GIVER OF UNMERITED FAVOR AND GRACE
ABLE TO ACCOMPLISH MORE IN A MOMENT THAN I CAN IN A LIFETIME
HAPPY TO ADVOCATE FOR ME
GREATER
MORE
LOVER OF MY SOUL
SOVEREIGN
CREATOR OF SOMETHING OUT OF NOTHING
FREE-ER FROM ENDLESS, EMPTY, ENTANGLING, DISAPPOINTING PERFORMANCE

MY DEFENDER

At times, I would write several at a time. Sometimes I wouldn't add to the list for weeks. Sometimes they were specific names mentioned in scripture...

EL-ELYON- MOST HIGH GOD
EL-SHADDAI- ALL SUFFICIENT ONE
ADONAI- LORD AND MASTER
JEHOVAH RAPHA- THE GOD WHO HEALS
JEHOVAH ROHI- THE LORD MY SHEPHERD
ELOHIM- CREATOR

Other times the list would so clearly reflect what I was walking and how the LOVING REVEALER OF HIMSELF was speaking into that moment...

ALL I WILL EVER NEED TO COMPLETE EVERYTHING YOU ARE ASKING OF ME
HE WHO SAYS, "LOVELY," WHEN I SAY, "BROKEN"
FEAR ZAPPER
WHO I CHOOSE WHEN I DON'T UNDERSTAND
HE WHO CALLS ME TO DANCE ON THE CLIFF WITH HIM WHEN FEAR STALKS
HE WHO WASTES NOT ONE EXPERIENCE BUT TURNS ALL TO OUR GOOD

Year after year, season after season.... The GENTLE BREEZE just kept blowing. The SOOTHING VOICE kept pointing out

His Presence. I just kept adding to that list. The treasure hunt wasn't always my consuming focus. It was just a part of my day by day walk with my MASTER. The list kept growing. It is still growing today. Sometimes I would read over that list when I was overwhelmed and needed to be reminded of the character of MY CONSTANT COMPANION. Sometimes I would pray some of those characteristics or names over myself, my family, hard situations, or hurting people I knew. I found myself beginning my prayer time calling out some of my favorite characteristics every day. As I told MY KING, "I am not repeating these out of vain repetition or because you need to be reminded Who You are. I am repeating them to remind myself Who I am talking to before I begin." I began to notice the absolute power in His character. As I meditated on Who He was, I found myself in absolute AWE. As I called out His character, I found myself near. As I drew near, I found Him revealing more of Himself. As He revealed more, I found myself craving. As I craved, He became TRUE SATISFACTION. As He became MY FULL FOCUS, I could exhale. And TRUE LOVE washed over me!

> *Psalm 75:1- "We give thanks to You, O God, we give thanks. For Your Name is near; Men declare Your wondrous works."*

> *Psalm 73:28- "But as for me, the nearness of God is my good; I have made the Lord God my refuge, that I may tell of all Your works."*

> *James 4:8-" Draw near to God and He will draw near to you. Cleanse your hands, you sinners; and purify your hearts, you double-minded."*

FAITHFUL LOVE was just getting started. I had been keeping my list for several years when He sent another GENTLE BREEZE love invitation. I was reading a devotional book by Vonette Bright, co-founder of Campus Crusade for Christ. In one of the devotionals, she encouraged readers to read the Psalms and take note of all the ways you see GOD's love.[14] A dear friend had just given me a beautiful journal with the words, "Called to Love," on the front. I thought this would be a fun study, so I began reading Psalms. When I would see a verse that pointed to His love, I would write the verse in my new journal. Something interesting began to happen, I started noticing GOD's character or name in those verses. Soon I was writing above each verse, Who He was revealing Himself to be in that verse. Slowly, the MASTER TEACHER was showing me the link between His character or name and His love. He was loving me with Himself...GOD was giving GOD. LOVE had a name. Actually.... LOVE has over 300 names...and that is just in the first half of the book of Psalms....

SHIELD ABOUT ME
MY GLORY
LIFTER OF MY HEAD
ANSWERER
SUSTAINER
HEARER OF MY CALLS
CONSTANT
AWESOME
ABUNDANT LOVINGKINDNESS
RESCUER OF MY SOUL
AWARE

INTIMATE
GIVER OF FAVOR
TRUSTWORTHY

Little did I realize.... those lists...they were His invitation to the love affair of all time. They were His call for me to come and know HIM. How can you be in love with someone you don't really even know? I thought I was just making an interesting list. Actually, He was seeping into my soul and I was being transformed.

2 Corinthians 3:18 says,
"But we all with unveiled face, beholding as in a mirror the glory of the Lord, are being transformed into the same image from glory to glory, just as from the Lord, the Spirit."

I had asked for a one time experience...a feeling... like a love zap. HE gave and continues to give me a daily encounter... like a tidal wave of HIMSELF. And no matter how many days I come, there is MORE. I have barely scratched the surface. He loves me with all He is. He loves you with all He is. Why? I can't fathom or explain it. It is just Who HE is! Take a minute and go back through the book so far. Slowly read the characteristics and names in all capital letters. Let them seep into your soul. This is just a small glimpse of the PEARL OF GREAT PRICE. This is the LOVER OF YOUR SOUL. This is how He loves. GOD gives GOD, and you can exhale. Precious ones, He is calling you to know Him and love Him. I get so excited knowing this is just a glimpse of all He wants to show you of Himself. Get ready for a TRUE LOVE ENCOUNTER. You will never be the same!

Chapter Eight:

A TREASURE Greater than the Blessings We Seek

But just as it is written, 'Things which eye has not seen
and ear has not heard, and which have not entered the heart
of man, all that God has prepared for those who love Him.'
For to us God revealed them through the Spirit;
for the Spirit searches all things, even the depths of God.
1 Corinthians 2:9-10

Would you humor me a moment and let me share a few stories from the "olden days".... otherwise known as my childhood? When I was a little girl, I would make my Christmas list and wake up with great expectations on Christmas morning hoping to find what I had requested. How I loved finding some of the gifts I asked to receive under the tree. However, those items I had requested weren't my favorites. My favorite gifts were the ones my mom called, "Surprises." Mom would always include at least one thing I didn't ask to receive. One year it was a child's typewriter with a note typed from Santa. One year it was a clock radio (which was a big deal before cell phones). One year it was a bicycle radio and horn that connected right on my butterfly handlebars!! That gift was incredible!! I remember thinking, "How can she know I want this when I didn't even know it existed, much less that I really wanted it?"

Mom was not the only one with the ability to read minds. One of my favorite memories of my dad happened on my first day of softball practice in the fifth grade. We had moved to Houston that year so I was the new girl. For some reason I can't remember, my parents signed me up to play softball. I had never played. Apparently in Houston, they began playing softball at two years old, so my ten year old self was ..... terrible. I came home from the first practice, and dad asked how it had gone. I remember bursting into tears and saying, "Daddy, I am the worst one. I don't even have a glove." I will forever love what my dad did in that moment. He put me in the car, and we were off to K-mart. He bought me a glove, a ball, a bat, and he even discussed a pitching net which I told him I didn't think was necessary. He practiced with me. It really wasn't about the glove (though forty-six years later I still have it in my attic). I didn't know what I needed, but he saw it. I needed confidence. I needed someone to see my weakness, join with me, equip me, and just be present. I needed him. How could he know what I needed when I didn't even know myself?

Precious ones, I am asking the GREAT TEACHER to help me put into words in the next few chapters the exponential number of "bicycle radios" and "Kmart trips" I have experienced with GOD THE BELOVED FATHER. How can He know what we really want when we ourselves don't realize how desperately we are hoping for something? How can He know what we need when we are so completely unaware of our deepest needs? How can He so lovingly listen to our prayers and so wisely sort through them to give us.... HIMSELF. I cannot answer these questions, but I can tell you with the greatest of assurance that there is a TREASURE so much greater than the blessings we seek.

How can we miss OUR INHERITANCE OF GREATEST VALUE, the TRUE DESIRE OF OUR HEART, the FULFILLMENT OF EVERY MISSING PIECE? How do we miss the TRUE TREASURE OF OUR SOULS? Quite honestly, I think it is the same issue Adam and Eve faced in the Garden. Do you remember the sin that started it all and remains the true root of all sin? "I will decide what is right and wrong for myself." Though at salvation we repented from the life of choosing what is right and wrong for ourselves, sometimes it seems our prayers and our expectations of the GREAT I AM still reflect the aroma of that raucous self-rule. And often like little children, we pout and declare our SOVEREIGN KING to be unjust, uncaring, untrustworthy, or not hearing when He, in HIS INFINITE WISDOM, dares to give us something different than we imagined... when He offers ... a TRUE GLIMPSE OF HIS GLORY.

As Paul E. Miller explains in *A Praying Life*, "I make the jump from optimism to darkness so quickly because I am not grounded in a deep, abiding faith that God is in the matter, no matter what the matter is. I am looking for pleasant results, not deeper realities."[15] How often do we unknowingly miss the TREASURE WE SO DESPERATELY NEED because we are fully mesmerized by the bauble of immediate comfort? How often does He ache because there HE stood, EVERYTHING WE NEED TO BE COMPLETE, and we couldn't see around our personal agenda long enough to catch a glimpse? C.S. Lewis explained our distraction this way, "It would seem that our LORD finds our desires not too strong, but too weak. We are half-hearted creatures, fooling about with drink and sex and ambition when INFINITE JOY is offered us, like an ignorant child who wants to go on making mud pies in a slum because he cannot imagine what is meant by the offer of a holiday at the sea. We are far too easily pleased."[16]

What if He offered us everything we asked for here on earth ... without His presence.... would we take the deal?

Moses had that very opportunity in Exodus 33. THE GREAT I AM had used Moses to lead His people from the slavery of Egypt moving toward the abundance of the Promised Land. They had seen miracle after miracle as their GREAT DELIVERER had split the Red Sea to allow them to pass, their CAPTAIN OF ANGEL ARMIES had defeated their enemies, their MIRACULOUS PROVIDER had sent food directly from heaven, their MAKER OF STREAMS IN THE DESERT had made drinking water flow from a rock, and their GREAT SHEPHERD had led every step. ALMIGHTY GOD called Moses up to the mountain to receive direction for His people. The people were to wait. They couldn't immediately see what GOD was doing. So they took matters into their own hands and put their agenda into place... sacrificing to and worshipping a god made with their own hands. Worse yet, they denied their DEFENDER and declared their plan to be the source of their freedom. Destruction loomed as the only recourse. Moses interceded. They were spared. Then came the chilling offer.

The KEEPER OF PROMISES and MAKER OF A WAY would send His angel army before them to clear their enemies. They would walk into the abundant Promised Land that He had promised He would give them. They would have the blessings they craved. There was only one thing. His EVER PRESENT, COMPASSIONATE, ALL-KNOWING, ALL-POWERFUL, ALWAYS PROVIDING PRESENCE wouldn't go with them. Just let that soak in for a minute. He offered them what our prayers and attitudes so often reflect.... "You can have the blessings, but you won't have Me." Be still and honest right now. Really reflect. Would you accept the offer? If He said, "You can have the great job, the new house, the relationship, the popularity, the scholarship, the grades, the applause, the fame, the "American Dream"... but you won't get the FULL TREASURE of Me." Do we even know what we would be missing? Would we even notice?

Moses knew what was at stake. Moses had a history of intimacy with the CONSUMING FIRE WHO CALLS ME TO COME CLOSE that was so RADIANT it left others craving and worshipping and desiring to linger in the presence of the LORD. Moses knew the ALMIGHTY GOD who was also his FRIEND.

Exodus 33:9-11
"Whenever Moses entered the tent, the pillar of cloud would descend and stand at the entrance of the tent; and the Lord would speak with Moses. When all the people saw the pillar of cloud standing at the entrance of the tent, all the people would arise and worship, each at the entrance of his tent. Thus the Lord used to speak to Moses face to face, just as a man speaks to his friend. When Moses returned to the camp, his servant

Joshua, the son of Nun, a young man, would not depart from the tent."

Moses' response to having all the presents without the PRECIOUS PRESENCE....

Exodus 33:15-16
"Then he said to Him, 'If Your Presence does not go with us, do not lead us up from here. For how then can it be known that I have found favor in Your sight, I and Your people? Is it not by Your going with us, so that we, I and Your people, may be distinguished from all the other people who are upon the face of the earth?"

Moses' response... "Noooo!!! Everything without You is absolutely nothing! You are OUR FAVOR, OUR DEFINER, OUR DISTINGUISHER, OUR VERY IDENTITY, OUR EVERYTHING!!"

Moses knew from experience that there was a TRANSCENDING TREASURE with layer after layer of GLORY to be revealed. He knew the TRANSFORMATIONAL POWER of that PRESENCE. No earthly trinket or position was worth that trade. HE was HOME. And when GOD gives GOD, we take off our shoes in joyful adoration and join Moses right there.

How can THE GREAT REVEALER OF HIS GLORY know exactly what we wanted when we didn't realize it ourselves? How can THE GREAT SHEPHERD OF OUR DESTINY know exactly what we needed when we couldn't put our ache into words? Could it be we are asking for blessings while He is trying to give us the blessing of Himself? My precious ones, there is a TREASURE so much GREATER than the blessings we seek. May we throw aside the fool's gold of our own agenda and run with all we are into the DIVINE PRESENCE of TRUE ETERNAL LIFE!

John 17:3-
"This is eternal <u>life</u>, that they may <u>know You</u>, the only true God, and Jesus Christ whom You have sent."

And as you run into His arms each day like little children on Christmas morning, you will find some glorious "surprises" under the tree of His LOVE. Like Paul prayed for his beloved children in the faith, I am praying the following for you...my most beloved ones...

Ephesians 1:15-23-
" For this reason I too, having heard of the faith in the Lord Jesus which exists among you and your love for all the saints, do not cease giving thanks for you, while making mention of you in my prayers; that the God of our Lord Jesus Christ, the Father of glory, may give you a spirit of <u>wisdom and of revelation in the knowledge of Him</u>. I pray that <u>the eyes of your heart may be enlightened</u>, so that you will <u>know</u> what is the <u>hope</u> of His calling, what are the <u>riches of the glory of His inheritance</u> in the saints, and what is the <u>surpassing greatness of His power toward us who believe</u>. These are in accordance with the working of the strength of His might which He brought about in Christ, when He raised Him from the dead and seated Him at His right hand in the heavenly places, <u>far above all rule and authority and power and dominion, and</u>

every name that is named, not only in this age but also in the one to come. And He put all things in subjection under His feet, and gave Him as head over all things to the church, which is His body, the fullness of Him who fills all in all."

May you expectantly and joyously open surprises like wisdom, revelation, hope, value, strength, power, fullness, and so much more ... all wrapped in the GLORIOUS NAME FAR ABOVE EVERY NAME... the GREAT TREASURE. GOD will give you GOD!!! You can exhale!

WORTHY - A Declaration of Love and Surrender
Prayer Journal

Take off your shoes
Fall on your face
For HE is in the room
And He is WORTHY!

Feel the weight of His GLORY
Smell the aroma of FREEDOM
Hear the call to RELEASE
WORTHY, WORTHY, WORTHY!

The BELOVED comes near
Hear the hushed silence
Heart racing anticipation
Crowns thrown at His feet
WORTHINESS!

He reigns, He completes, He rescues
He requires, He gives all that is required
He loves, He embraces, He gathers up close.
And the closer we get, the harder it is to breathe
yet the easier it is to exhale
WORTHY , WORTHY , WORTHY!

WORTHY , WORTHY , WORTHY!
Of all my love, all my life, of wholly and totally all!
Chosen, Beloved, His, Treasured- how can it be
Such GRACE, such PURPOSE, so much MORE
Oh praise the ONE AND ONLY WORTHY KING
MY BELOVED, MY SAVIOR, MY ALL!!!

I love you LORD, truly, with all my heart! You are WORTHY!!

Chapter Nine:

The Blessing

Then the LORD spoke to Moses, saying,
'Speak to Aaron and to his sons, saying, Thus you shall
bless the sons of Israel, You shall say to them:
The LORD bless you, and keep you;
The LORD make His face shine on you,
And be gracious to you,
The LORD lift up His countenance on you
And give you peace.
So they shall invoke My Name on the sons of Israel,
and I then will bless them.'
Numbers 6:22-27

Blessings. We often think of "blessings" as getting wonderful
things from God... health, family, success, good weather...
and receiving those things makes us "blessed." Though His
gifts are wonderful and I am beyond grateful for their presence
in my life, Numbers 6 describes a different type of blessing. The

TRUE BLESSING instructs the priests to speak this blessing over His people prior to entering the Promised Land. The GREAT PROVIDER will give them many wonderful gifts in the Promised Land. The GIVER OF ALL GOOD THINGS literally described it as **"a land flowing with milk and honey."** The gifts will be there, but the BLESSER wants to give them more. He wants to give them HIMSELF. Note the central focus of the blessing on the sons of Israel in Numbers 6.... the LORD...His keeping... the LORD...His face... the LORD...His countenance. And notice the beautiful result of God's blessing.... **"So they shall invoke My Name on the sons of Israel, and I then will bless them."** As they call for more of Him, His Name will settle on them. That is the ultimate blessing. Oh the beauty of the blessing of His Name... of His Character... of His Glory!

Beloved, there is so much more to this idea of blessing than we may have imagined. As a matter of fact, blessing as it pertains to our relationship with GOD was intended to be a two-way intimacy. GOD blesses us with His Name, and we bless His Name with all we are. This may be one of the key secrets to this love affair we have been describing throughout the book.

Throughout all of scripture, there are calls for us to bless the LORD.

> **Psalm 103:1-**
> *"Bless the LORD, O my soul, and all that is within me, bless His holy name."*

> **Psalm 104:1-**
> *"Bless the Lord, O my soul! O Lord my God, You are very great;*

You are clothed with splendor and majesty."

Daniel 2:20–
"Daniel said, 'Let the name of God be blessed forever and ever. For wisdom and power belong to Him.'"

Ephesians 1:3–
"Blessed be the God and Father of our Lord Jesus Christ, Who has blessed us with every spiritual blessing in the heavenly places in Christ."

He blesses me and I bless Him. How can I... in all my finiteness... bless the POSSESSOR OF ALL and GIVER OF ALL BLESSINGS? What does it truly mean to bless? In his book, *Double Blessing*[17], Mark Batterson discusses six meanings of the word, *barak*, which is the Hebrew word for bless. As I studied the meanings, I was so moved by the depth of blessing ALMIGHTY GOD was offering His people. As I looked in amazement at how GOD desired to bless us, I felt the nudge of the WHISPERER to pause and look at each meaning of *barak* Batterson explored and also consider how we as finite humans could *barak* Him back.

Meaning of *Barak* How He Blesses Us	How We Bless Him
"to salute" Reveals Himself and welcomes us	Look to Him with transparency and surrender
"to kneel down" Kneels down in "withness" with us	Come excitedly to meet with Him
"to kiss on the lips" Resuscitates us	Worship and truly adore Him
"to speak words of excellence about" Speaks life over us	Praise Him profusely
"to make peace" Authors our peace	Abide in His love and peace
"to cause to prosper" Gives all we need	Exalt and serve

As I was studying the beautiful depth of *barak*... blessing...,
the SPIRIT guided me to Psalm 134. Beloved ones, don't miss
this part for it is the true secret to the transforming....day after
day, month after month, year after year,... beyond all ability to
comprehend or explain...love affair with the CREATOR OF YOUR
HEART and REDEEMER OF YOUR SOUL.

Psalm 134:1-2-
*"Behold, bless the LORD, all servants of the LORD, who serve
(stand) by night in the house of the LORD! Lift up your hands
to the sanctuary (apartness/sacredness) and bless the LORD."*

Every day and every moment, the DIRECTOR OF THE
DIVINE ROMANCE invites me to... bless Him... to lift my eyes
to His EYES OF COMPASSION and my hands to His throne
to worship His HOLINESS. He bids me to come with full
transparency and absolute surrender... no need to hide my
feelings, deny my fears, cover my failures, word my questions
just right, or pretend I have no doubts. The UNCONDITIONAL
LOVER longs for me to come excitedly... just like I am ...to bring it
all to Him. He can handle it. The INTIMATE KING already knows.
MY CONSTANT is not rattled or even surprised by my weakness.
Somehow what repulses others seems to draw Him.

Like fine perfume mingled with tears, I can pour out my
worship and adoration and time and love, and I can praise MY
REDEEMING BRIDEGROOM profusely. And I choose to stay...
to abide... to dwell... right there in His FAITHFUL LOVE and
INEXPLICABLE PEACE. I begin to call out and exalt and bask in
all those descriptors of His character...His GLORIOUS POWERFUL

NAME ..all right here with me in this moment. I find myself hungry to give Him all. I find myself in AWE.... amazed by the enormity of His character, wonderstruck by the beauty of His ways, enraptured by the reality of His presence.

But that is just the first part of the encounter described in Psalm 134.

Psalm 134:3-
"May the LORD bless you from Zion (the dwelling place of God and center of His people), He who made heaven and earth."

For as I bless Him, the INCOMPREHENSIBLE GOD OF THE UNIVERSE blesses me. Somehow the TREASURER OF HIS PEOPLE sees my frame and hears my voice, and ADORING LOVE graciously and knowingly turns His face toward me....to welcome... me...to reveal more of Himself to ... me. How can that be? He seems to smile as He leads me to uncover another multi-karat jewel of the zillion-karat jewel of His MIND BLOWING ESSENCE... EMMANUEL- GOD WITH US...He knew I would love that one. And as He reveals His HEALING WITHNESS, I experience it all over again. He is HERE and He is WITH ME and I can somehow catch my breath and exhale. His AWESOMENESS washes over all the heavy and all the hard, and the BREATH OF LIFE resuscitates me. And the GREAT PARACLETE-THE ONE CALLED BESIDE ME...speaks LIFE over me.... the ETERNAL LIFE of Who HE is and who that makes me.

He is LOVER... I am loved. He is ALL SEEING... I am not invisible. He is ENOUGH... I can stop striving. He is the GOOD SHEPHERD ... I can follow and trust. He is MORE... the scary must silence. He is UNCHANGING and UNSTOPPABLE... the world is not shaking. He is FATHER... I am protected. He is PROVIDER... I am not lacking. And as I bask in amazement at His AWESOMENESS, the WONDERFUL COUNSELOR lifts His countenance on me and ushers in PEACE. And all the voices yelling in my head when I entered are silenced at the mention of His NAME ABOVE ALL NAMES. My needs are met. I am most well off. For GOD has given GOD and I am truly blessed!!

Beloved ones, this is not a one time dance of blessing. This is your birthright as His child every moment of every day... to come to Him with blessing and find yourself immeasurably blessed with Him. LIMITLESS GOD will never run out of ways to bless you with the revelation of Himself. Never! Just come and ask. Do you want to know more of Him? Ask. Do you want to love Him more? Ask. Come as you... not as anyone else. It really is silly that we think we have to all look the same in His Presence. If we are made new in JESUS... the DOOR is wide open. He isn't looking for flowery words or memorized prayers. Your time with Him may not look anything like anyone else's time with Him. He isn't looking for you to have your act all together and your doctrine all in line. He will take care of all that. He doesn't need your service. The SELF-EXISTENT and SELF-SUFFICIENT ONE doesn't need a thing. He just wants you to bring you with a hungry heart, and He will bring Himself and then... brace yourself. You may just find yourself lavishly loved and... blessed!

2/16/2021.... Prayer Journal

LORD,

Sometimes trying to grasp the DIVINE ENORMITY of You with the immense weakness of me leaves me rattled and trying to cling with my mind darting like a ping pong ball. But then, You speak... a word, a phrase, a verse... just enough for me to hold on to. It is like how I try to teach Jane to speak..." ball "..."flower"... " hot." I repeat those little bits You give and You applaud- pleased with the effort, blessed by the focus, encouraged by the imitation. And I find GRACE- the GRACE that doesn't expect me to get it all right- but willingly makes it manageable and celebrates the growth. Oh Lord, hold me here with the little one-karat portion of the zillion-karat TREASURE of You. And thank You, Lord, that You gave everything to purchase the digging rights for me to the sweetest diamond mine of all time. Make me Your most dedicated miner. For in beholding the TREASURE... even the smallest portion of the TREASURE...I am transformed!!

I love you, BELOVED,
Your Kelli..forever

Chapter Ten:

Show Me Your GLORY

Right now you may be thinking, "I would love to have a blessing encounter with the LOVING GOD you describe, but right now I am really struggling to see Him that way." Oh beloved one, I totally understand. Please don't let my description of time with HE WHO BESTOWS HIMSELF mislead you to believe that every day in every moment I experience the euphoric realization of His Presence where I can all but hear the *Hallelujah Chorus*[18] in the background. This would not be true. As I will describe for you later in the book, He revealed Himself most when I was most in need. I discovered Him as ABUNDANTLY PRESENT IN EVERY DAY AND EVERY CIRCUMSTANCE on days I was unsure, terrified, and looking everywhere for relief. I discovered Him as GIVER OF FAVOR EVEN WHEN IT HURTS when I was walking hard things that seemed to go on and on but were somehow designed to conform me to His image. I discovered Him as GOOD SHEPHERD when I was walking great loss and so desperately needed comfort. He became HE WHO

CLOTHES ME IN HIS STRENGTH AND WRAPS ME IN HIS PEACE when I was anything but strong and far from peaceful. He revealed Himself as PROVIDER when bills outlived paychecks, and I felt fully desperate.

You see, beloved, I think sometimes if we were really honest, we might say we are finding it hard to bless GOD as GOOD because we look around our lives, our families, our communities, and our world and we see so much that is ... bad. We may not say it out loud, but we are finding it hard to draw near in utter surrender when everything seems so out of control.

I understand.

My list of His MAJESTY includes HE WHO BIDS ME TO LOSE CONTROL (EVEN IN YOUR RELATIONSHIP WITH ME) and HE WHO SOMETIMES WITHHOLDS RESULTS SO I TRUST HIM WITH OR WITHOUT THEM and WHO I CHOOSE WHEN I DON'T UNDERSTAND and HE IN WHOM I AM NOT OFFENDED- REGARDLESS OF LIFE- BECAUSE I TRUST. I am sure you can imagine the encounters where HE WHO KNOWS BEST blessed me with those parts of HIMSELF. I am not being facetious. He truly blessed me with those jewels as well. I am forever grateful for those gifts. But they were not easy jewels to mine.

Sometimes I struggle with a GOD I can't fully understand or explain. Perhap, like me, you struggle with the great... and ... of INFINITE GOD. Let me explain that a little further. OUR GOD is both MERCIFUL and JUST. I have to really stretch my human brain not to see those as opposites. When I look at them with my finite understanding, I sometimes wonder if His mercy is unjust or His justice is unmerciful. He is also SOVEREIGN and the GIVER OF CHOICE. How can He be both? Add to this that sometimes the LORD GOD OF RECOMPENSE in the Old Testament acts in ways I can't explain and find a bit frightening. Some churches proclaim Him exclusively as the LOVING FRIEND and others weekly proclaim Him as RIGHTEOUS JUDGE. By the way, scripture says He is both... another great... and. And in case you haven't noticed, our world constantly describes Him as narrow-minded, full of hate, and culturally irrelevant. Perhaps you don't know how to reconcile all the sides of the OMNI-FACETED TREASURE so you find yourself ... distant.

Oh precious one, you are not alone. Just a few weeks ago, I found myself in just that spot. Yes, there are times when I am spending time with GOD, I feel so close it almost seems I could touch Him. And yes, there are times I struggle and wonder if I even know Him at all. I believe that is why they call it faith. Just a few weeks ago, I was wrestling, and I was completely miserable. I was wrestling with all the bad news and wrestling with the varying explanations of the ALMIGHTY... and I don't know how I found myself there, but I do know it felt dark and alone and I couldn't seem to wrap my mind or heart around TRUTH.

One thing I have learned in my fifty year dance with the INCONCEIVABLE is that the worst thing I can do when I am struggling is to stop coming. The enemy of my soul wins in that scenario. But if I will continue to come and ask with an open heart, LIGHT IN THE DARKNESS will break through. If I really want revelation (and not just confirmation that I am right), the SPIRIT OF TRUTH will lead me to SOUL REST even in the absence of human intellectual understanding. It may take some time, and I may have to wait, but He will lead me to the ROCK ON WHICH I STAND. I can't wrestle these hard to understand things for you.

Faith is a personal wrestle, but I can share with you what the GUARD AND POSSESSOR OF MY HEART showed me.

> **Romans 8:18-25-**
> *" For I consider that the sufferings of this present time are not worthy to be compared with the glory that is to be revealed to us. For the anxious longing of the creation waits eagerly for the revealing of the sons of God. For the creation was subjected to futility, not willingly, but because of Him who subjected it, in hope that the creation itself also will be set free from its slavery to corruption into the freedom of the glory of the children of God. For we know that the whole creation groans and suffers the pains of childbirth together until now. And not only this, but also we ourselves, having the first fruits of the Spirit, even we ourselves groan within ourselves, waiting eagerly for our adoption as sons, the redemption of our body. For in hope we have been saved, but hope that is seen is not hope; for who hopes for what he already sees? But if we hope for what we do not see, through perseverance we wait eagerly for it. "*

The first glimmer of LIGHT came as the GUIDE led me to grasp again the full impact man's rebellion against CREATOR GOD had on all creation. As John Piper explained in a message on Romans 8:18-25, SOVEREIGN GOD subjected all creation to futility with the audacity of man's fall. Futility means nothing works as it is supposed to work... enter disease, famine, hurt, brokenness. Nothing works as it should because man rejected the GIVER OF LIFE. RESCUING GOD subjected all to futility in hopes that the brokenness would awaken us to the horrors of exchanging His GLORY for other things. All creation groans awaiting the day when all is set right again. We groan as well. For though we have the taste of RESTORATION in our communion with the SPIRIT, we are impacted by the futility until REDEEMING GOD... LONGSUFFERING GOD... calls us to our real home.[19]

> Romans 8:26-30-
> *"In the same way the Spirit also helps our weakness; for we do not know how to pray as we should, but the Spirit Himself intercedes for us with groanings too deep for words; and He who searches the hearts knows what the mind of the Spirit is, because He intercedes for the saints according to the will of God. And we know that God causes all things to work together for good to those who love God, to those who are called according to His purpose. For those whom He foreknew, He also predestined to become conformed to the image of His Son, so that He would be the firstborn among many brethren; and these whom He predestined, He also called; and these whom He called, He also justified; and these whom He justified, He also glorified."*

And while His children wait, haunted and impacted by the futility of it all, the VERY SPIRIT OF GOD HIMSELF intercedes for them with aching and groaning prayers. The GOD WHO WASTES NOTHING causes all the hard to conform them to the image of HIS BELOVED SON. And the FAITHFUL TO COMPLETE THE WORK leads them to glory. He wastes nothing... even the hard... the very hard.

I saw it. Why was I shocked when the brokenness and curse of futility... the hurt, the evil, the chaos, the confusion, nothing being quite like it should be... touched His children, too? We are citizens of earth. Earth is broken. Sometimes the effects of the brokenness rock us to the core. How do we handle those aches?

John 16:33-
"These things I have spoken to you, so that in Me you may have peace. In the world you have tribulation, but take courage; I have overcome the world."

We take courage because we know the OVERCOMING KING is in the process of setting things back in order. SUBSTITUTIONARY ATONEMENT was His idea. REGENERATION is His calling card. RECONCILIATION is His heart's cry. SOVEREIGN GOD could have made a different choice. He could have left us enslaved to our own choice. The whole reason JESUS came was to activate REDEMPTION in the midst of all this brokenness. For now, the whole earth is subjected to futility and things don't work like they are supposed to work... even for believers. Sometimes the effects seem to break our hearts and challenge our hope. What then?

We lock eyes. We lock eyes with the IMMOVABLE. We trust that ETERNAL FATHER is very aware and close to hold His dear ones through the hard. We lean on the PRINCE OF PEACE Who is there to offer inexplicable peace when we are not immediately freed from hurt. We tune our ears to hear the COMFORTER lovingly assure us that nothing is wasted... nothing. This is faith.

Yet, I still found myself struggling. Why didn't

OMNIPOTENT GOD do it all a different way? The LAMP TO MY FEET next took me back to Moses and His GLORY ENCOUNTER in Exodus 33. If you will remember from the last chapter, Moses refused to lead the people forward without the Presence of GOD. He interceded on behalf of the rebellious people for the DELIVERER to go with them. MERCIFUL GOD agreed. Now Moses comes to HOLY GOD with a request of his own. You know what I love about Moses? It wasn't just about ministry for Moses, and he wasn't content to think he had GOD all figured out for himself. He craved MORE... not just so he could lead better... he wanted MORE for himself. Let me take you through this conversation and give a little commentary in light of how GOD used it in my wrestling...

> **Exodus 33:18–**
> *"Then Moses said, 'I pray You, show me Your glory!'"*
>> Moses cries out, "LORD, I want more of YOU for me."

> **Exodus 33:19–23–**
> *"And HE said, "I, Myself"*
>> I love the personalness of this. GOD HIMSELF will reveal His GLORY to Moses and to us.

> *"will make all My goodness pass before you"*
>> The REVEALER OF HIS NATURE reveals and awakens us to His GOODNESS. GOD'S GLORY begins with His GOODNESS,

> *"and will proclaim the Name of the LORD before you"*
>> Notice that when Moses asked to see the GLORY of

GOD, GOD proclaims His Name. His Name declares His Character, and embedded in His Character is His GLORY. This might be a good time to go back through all His Names and character traits in this book so far. Remember that is just the fringe of His ways. I believe you will get a glimpse of GLORY.

"and I will be gracious to whom I will be gracious, and will show compassion on whom I will show compassion"

This was a key point for me. This was where I was struggling. GOD's message? GOD reveals His SOVEREIGNTY. Basically the message here is, "I get to be GOD."

Notice that before this GOD has promised He will allow His GOODNESS to pass and His Name to be declared. Here was the question I heard in my spirit at this point, "On the foundation of my GOODNESS and in light of Who My Name declares me to be... can you trust My SOVEREIGNTY? Can you be at peace with the fact that you are finite in your understanding and I am INFINITE in My WISDOM and rest in letting Me be GOD...even if you don't understand?"

"But He said, "You cannot see My face, for no man can see My face and live!""

Here God reveals our limitedness. He basically says, "Finite you can't handle all there is of INFINITE Me. It would kill you if I showed you all of it. You are going to have to trust Me on this."

Here I had to just stop and ask myself if I really wanted a GOD I could fully explain and control. Would that really be GOD or would that make us equal? Isn't that desire what started all of this futility in the first place? Could I trust that me not understanding all of it was actually proof He was INCOMPREHENSIBLE? Could I trust His heart that He was protecting me? Could I accept that GOD gets to be GOD and doesn't answer to me? The only alternative was for me to be my own god. We will look at the bleakness of that choice in a few minutes.

> *"Then the Lord said, 'Behold, there is a place by (with) Me, and you shall stand there on the rock;"*
> I absolutely love this part. GOD invites us to intimacy as our solid foundation. GOD basically says, "I get to be GOD, but there is a place NEAR Me, you can stand right there.. Just keep coming in close. You can be WITH me. Withness is where you will stand immovable."

RELATIONAL GOD invites us to draw near and be WITH Him.

> *"and it will come about, while My GLORY is passing by, that I will put you in the cleft of the rock and cover you with My hand until I have passed by. Then I will take My hand away and you shall see My back, but My face shall not be seen."*
> I love this, too. God promises to lovingly protect us in our dance with Him and His transforming GLORY. In other words, ALL CONSUMING GOD realizes we will struggle to grasp all of His ways. LOVING GOD helps us and protects us through our struggles to embrace

INFINITE SOVEREIGNTY with our little cup of finiteness.

As I read this, I knew it was true because I had just experienced the reality of the dance.

In my struggle to grasp LIMITLESS GOD, I ultimately find myself with two choices. I can accept that GOD gets to be GOD, embrace my own finiteness, and trust Him and His Character ... or...I can choose to be my own god, embrace my own significance, and depend on my own performance.

Let's take a brief look at that second choice...

Psalm 135:15-18
" The idols of the nations are but silver and gold, the work of man's hands."
> Our idols (the works of our hands) today look more like... performance, approval, success, intellectualism, reputation...

"They have mouths, but they do not speak; They have eyes but they do not see."
> Have you noticed those idols we make with our hands are constantly yelling for more yet never fully consoled or satisfied? Have you noticed that our idols seem to be constantly evaluating us on the outside but never really seeing us at our core?

"They have ears but they do not hear, nor is there any breath at all in their mouths. Those who make them will be like them, yes,

everyone who trusts in them."

Have you noticed our handmade idols of significance seem to judge by the letter with no regard for our heart or what we were trying to say or accomplish? Have you noticed those replacement gods give no long-lasting sustaining life? Have you noticed how harsh that internal and external critic can be?

Following this dismal discourse on gods made with the hands of man, the writer of Psalms seems to bellow out this plea...

Psalm 135:19-21
"O house of Israel, bless the LORD; O house of Aaron, bless the LORD; O house of Levi, bless the LORD; You who revere the LORD, bless the LORD. Blessed be the LORD from Zion, who dwells in Jerusalem. Praise the LORD!"

The writer begs..."bless the LORD, bless the LORD, bless the LORD..." He then moves to Psalm 136 where he recounts who the LORD is and what He has done interspersed with this one phrase repeated twenty-six times.....

"FOR HIS LOVINGKINDNESS IS EVERLASTING."

That seems to take us right back to where we started. I bless Him and He blesses me, and I am transformed by the EVERLASTING LOVE of SOVEREIGN GOD. All other gods... well... they are as empty and elusive as the golden calf the children of Israel danced around while Moses was up on the mountain blessing and being blessed with the GLORY OF GOD.

By the way, it was LAVISH LOVE that ultimately ended my recent struggle. After I had studied and analyzed all the verses and wailed to understand pain and suffering and sovereignty and choice... I heard that GENTLE BREEZE say ever so softly,

"You know, I love you unconditionally. Do you think you could do the same for ME?"

Well of course, MY BELOVED. Of course.

SECTION THREE:

Chronicles of Intimacy

Psalm 34:6-7-

"This poor man cried, <u>and the LORD heard him and saved him</u> out of all his troubles. The angel of the LORD encamps around those who fear Him, and rescues them."

Chapter Eleven:

In Every Season

Seasons. I have to admit, I think they are one of GOD's greatest ideas. I would have to say fall is my favorite. I just love fall leaves, apple cider, Thanksgiving, and everything pumpkin. But how do you discount winter, with its blanket of winter snow, snuggles in front of the fire, and the glory of Christmas? One of my best friends loves spring as green explodes onto the horizon, flowers erupt in color, and Easter services celebrate life. And what kind of educator would I be if I didn't love summer.... slow moving days, family vacations, time in the water, and in the best of scenarios sand between my toes?

But just like there are seasons of the year, my precious ones, there are also seasons of life. There are seasons of youth and seasons of aging. There are seasons of love and community and seasons of loneliness and hurt. There are seasons of success and accomplishment and seasons of confusion and defeat. There are seasons of growing families and seasons of family loss. There are seasons of health and fitness and seasons of illness and exhaustion. As invigorating as each of the different seasons of the year can be to our soul, dear ones, I wouldn't be honest at all if I didn't say seasons of life can sometimes leave our soul parched and bleeding and our faith tired and floundering. This may be a point where I need to apologize one more time for my generation. I think perhaps in our great desire to make everything positive and good for you, our dear children, we may have forgotten to tell you that life can be... very... hard. LIfe can change very quickly. Sometimes we see it coming. Sometimes we don't.

Now before you cover your head and refuse to get out of bed, let me tell you two life changing truths. The first one is this... JESUS never changes!

Hebrews 13:8 says,
"Jesus Christ is the same yesterday and today and forever."

Before you say to yourself, "Yeah, yeah, yeah I know JESUS doesn't change," go back a minute and slowly read the names and characteristics of GOD that are capitalized in this book. Let the weight of glory in each one seep into your soul, and realize that Who those words describe Him to be to you does not change.

Hebrews 6:17-20 says,
"In the same way God, desiring even more to show to the heirs of the promise the unchangeableness of His purpose, interposed with an oath, so that by two unchangeable things in which it is impossible for God to lie, we who have taken refuge would have strong encouragement to take hold of the hope set before us.

This hope we have as an anchor of the soul, a hope both sure and steadfast and one which enters within the veil, where Jesus has entered as a forerunner for us, having become a high priest forever according to the order of Melchizedek."

Wait...what is our SOURCE OF ENCOURAGEMENT and our HOPE ANCHOR when life leaves us flipped and change leaves us grasping for something that isn't moving? How do we cope when the world seems to be shifting or our personal life is so manic or so mundane we aren't sure we can face tomorrow? Our STRONGHOLD is that GOD doesn't change, GOD's purposes don't change, GOD doesn't lie, and because of JESUS we are welcomed to intimacy with GOD and the magnitude of HIS GREATNESS!!

I told you there were two life-changing truths I wanted to share. Here is the second one. Not only does JESUS not change, but....He is very involved in your season. One of my favorite books of all time is *A Shepherd Looks at Psalm 23* by W. Phillip Keller[20]. In his book, Keller describes the intimate and all consuming work the shepherd performs in taking his sheep through every season of the year. The shepherd has gone before preparing the way for each season, he stays with the sheep throughout each season, and he is always looking forward to the next season. The season you are in right now or the one you constantly fear is just around the corner...our GOOD SHEPHERD goes before you to that season to prepare the ground... our INTIMATE SHEPHERD walks with you in that season.... and our ALREADY THERE SHEPHERD knows what is coming, so there is nothing to fear. Sometimes when I get nervous about the coming season, I remind myself, "His LOVE will be there, too."

I tell you this, my beloved ones, because sometimes our fear gets so loud or our pain gets so intense that we don't see our PRECIOUS INVOLVED SHEPHERD right there. We might miss the incredible depth of His character He is trying to reveal to us. We might not recognize the enormous magnitude of His closeness in the season...until we look back. Or we might just forget to look back... and what He intended to be a chronicle of His intimacy with us instead becomes a litany of complaint and discouragement. Oh my precious ones, don't rob yourself. Don't miss Who He was, Who He is, and Who He will be... in this season... in every season. The enormity might just change your life... and your season.

Recently I did a study of what I call the "glory guys." These men are some of the heroes of the Bible who had very real encounters with the glory of GOD. I have already told you about several of them... Moses, Isaiah, Paul. But I have to admit, one of the glory guys who most ministers to me is Elijah. I love his story because my personality so relates to Elijah. Elijah's glory encounter comes while he is in a funk. That truth brings so much hope to my "easy to go into a funk" self. He has just seen GOD ALMIGHTY do an amazing work and literally send fire down from heaven. MIRACLE WORKING GOD has then broken a three year drought with a downpour and allowed Elijah to outrun a chariot. Sounds like a glorious season, doesn't it? But then, one woman's criticism leads to threats and the fearless prophet warrior becomes the fearful burned out cynic. Seasons are like that. Quite honestly, I am like that.

I think I love this story so much because in this season of

spiritual, emotional, and physical exhaustion, LOVING GOD is so.... TENDER. He doesn't angrily rebuke Elijah for forgetting Who He serves and being weak. As Elijah pours out his fears and frustration, his feelings of defeat and discouragement.... as he literally asks to die.... GENTLE LOVING GOD lets him sleep. CAREGIVING GOD sends angels to feed him. ALREADY KNOWING GOD asks, "What are you doing here, Elijah?" I love this for so many reasons. I love that INTIMATE GOD calls him by name. I love that LISTENING GOD basically says, "Tell me about it." I love that as Elijah pours out the realities of his season (at least his somewhat skewed perceptions of them), COMPASSIONATE GOD positions him for a glory sighting. SUCH LAVISH GRACE! The Bible says in 1 Kings 19:11 that Elijah is sent to stand on a mountain before the Lord and *"behold the LORD was passing by!"* If you know the story, you know there was a tornado-like wind, a rock breaking earthquake, and a burning fire.... but that wasn't where GOD was found. The GLORIOUS VOICE was in the gentle breeze. Yes, there HE is!!

So often, when a season leaves me spent and I just want to quit or stay in bed (I would be embarrassed, dear one, if you knew how many of those seasons I have allowed myself to encounter).... when my anxieties are blowing my security around like a tornado.... when the earth seems to be shifting and I can't find a stable place to stand... when the issues keep spreading like wildfire and I am convinced no one cares... GRACIOUS GOD calls me to the mountain of my knees and "behold the LORD is passing by!" THE GOD WHO KNOWS ME BY NAME lets me pour out my sometimes skewed perceptions of the season and He gently reveals Himself... again. I say again on purpose here.

Because you see, beloved ones, if in that moment I could take a moment to reflect on Who He has revealed Himself to be in all the past seasons of my life, I am pretty sure the apprehension about this current season or the coming season would bow to His MATCHLESS GREATNESS and UNFLINCHING LOVE. I would see the GOOD SHEPHERD right there in the midst.

One day as I was reflecting on this glory sighting in Eljah's life, I thought it would be interesting to put myself in Elijah's shoes and choose to look back on Who GOD had shown Himself to be in the seasons of Elijah's life prior to and after His glory encounter. Quite honestly, I was just awestruck. As I read the snapshots of Elijah's life in 1 Kings 17 through 2 Kings 2, I found that GOD had revealed over fifty characteristics of Himself to and through Elijah's life. And that is just in the stories we know. Humor me as I show you what I mean...

- Elijah's season as the prophet declaring the hard news of a coming drought and living through the three year drought- GOD revealed Himself as...
  - HIDER OF HIS OWN
  - MIRACULOUS PROVIDER
  - COMMANDER OF CREATION
  - OWNER OF ALL
  - AWARE OF NEED
  - AWARE OF PROVISION
  - LEADER TO ANSWERS
  - MULTIPLIER OF LITTLE
  - MULTI-TASKER
  - SEER OF ALL
  - CALLER TO RISKY FAITH

- KEEPER OF PROMISE
- MULTI-STRATEGY PROVIDER
- SOVEREIGN
- GIVER OF LIFE
- RAISER OF THE DEAD
- Elijah's season of confronting double-mindedness and false gods- GOD revealed Himself as...
  - LORD
  - GOD OF ABRAHAM, ISAAC, AND ISRAEL
  - GOD WHO REIGNS
  - MASTER AND CONFIRMER OF HIS SERVANTS
  - DECLARER OF THE WORD
  - INITIATOR
  - CONSUMING FIRE
  - ONE TRUE GOD
  - WORTHY OF WORSHIP
  - SUPPLIER OF SUPERNATURAL ENERGY
  - GIVER OF MORE
  - TRUE TO HIS WORD

- Elijah's season as an exhausted, fearful, depressed prophet- GOD revealed Himself as...
  - CONTROLLER OF LIFE
  - COMPASSIONATE
  - SEER OF WEAKENED STATE
  - TENDER PROVIDER
  - SENDER OF MINISTERING ANGELS
  - ALLOWER OF REST
  - GRACIOUS UNDERSTANDING

- · KNOWER OF OUR FRAME
- · CALLER TO MORE
- · PROVIDER OF NOURISHMENT FOR MORE
- · DECIDER OF FINISH LINE
- · POSITIONER FOR A GLORY SIGHTING
- · GOD
- · CHOOSER OF THE SIMPLE OR SPECTACULAR DISPLAY
- · GENTLE BLOWING CALL/ WOOER
- · FAMILIAR VOICE
- · REVEALER OF HEART AND MOTIVE

- Elijah's season of being called to his final mission– GOD revealed Himself as...
  - · CHOOSER OF LEADERS
  - · EXIT/ SUCCESSION PLANNER
  - · OWNER OF THE BATTLE
  - · CHOOSER OF THE WARRIORS
  - · KNOWER OF HIS REMNANT
  - · CHOOSER OF MENTEES AND MISSION
  - · PROVIDER OF SUPPORT
  - · LEGACY MAKER
  - · SENDER OF GLORIOUS TRANSPORT HOME

One life. Just a few snapshot seasons of that life. This is our AWESOME AND INTIMATE GOD. This is the HOLDER OF OUR SEASONS. This is our GREAT SHEPHERD. Doesn't He just leave you speechless?

Can I blow your mind just one more little bit? About a

month after this study, the GREAT REVEALER OF HIMSELF led me to look a little deeper at just one of the characteristics from Elijah's life. I was reading a devotional book by Cynthia Schneider that mentioned EL RACHUM, the Hebrew name for GOD that means COMPASSIONATE.[21] I chose to study places in scripture where His compassion is mentioned (Deuteronomy 4:31, Exodus 34:6, 2 Chronicles 30:9, Nehemiah 9:31, Psalm 103:8, Psalm 111:4, Psalm 116:5, Jonah 4:2). As I looked at the characteristics associated with just that one name, I was amazed. When we say we serve COMPASSIONATE GOD, we must realize His COMPASSION is...

- PRESENT AND WORKING
- FOR YOU
- REMEMBERING
- GRACE-SOAKED
- PATIENT
- ABOUNDING IN LOVINGKINDNESS (LOVE DOES)
- COMMITTED
- FORGIVING
- PROTECTIVE
- STAYING
- REMINDING
- SETTING THINGS RIGHT
- GRIEVING, SIGHING, SORRY OVER YOUR PAINFUL SITUATION

Do you see it, my dear ones? In one life with snapshots of just a few seasons, GOD reveals Himself in over fifty ways. If you take just one of those ways, GOD reveals Himself in ten more ways. Do you see that if you spent every second of your life listing a characteristic of the ENORMITY, LOVE, and CLOSENESS of GOD you would have barely scratched the surface? Do you understand why David couldn't help but exclaim...

Psalm 23:1– "The LORD is my shepherd, I shall not want."

In other words, He is HERE, and I lack nothing... in any season... even the hard ones... even this one!

His Eye is on the Sparrow
by Civilla D. Martin

Why should I feel discouraged, why should the shadows come,
Why should my heart be lonely, and long for heaven and home,
When Jesus is my portion? My constant friend is He:
His eye is on the sparrow, and I know He watches me;
His eye is on the sparrow, and I know He watches me.

"Let not your heart be troubled," His tender word I hear,
And resting on His goodness, I lose my doubts and fears;
Though by the path He leadeth, but one step I may see;
His eye is on the sparrow, and I know He watches me;
His eye is on the sparrow, and I know He watches me.

Whenever I am tempted, whenever clouds arise,
When songs give place to sighing, when hope within me dies,
I draw the closer to Him, from care He sets me free;

His eye is on the sparrow, and I know He watches me;
His eye is on the sparrow, and I know He watches me.
I sing because I'm happy,
I sing because I'm free,
For His eye is on the sparrow,
And I know He watches me. [22]

Chapter Twelve:

Keepsakes of Faithfulness

I f I announced in church we were going to begin a series on the book of Deuteronomy followed by our next series covering the books of First and Second Chronicles, people might not try to get there early to be sure they had a seat. But recently, the GREAT REMEMBERER has nudged me to take a look at the purposes of those books. Deuteronomy is believed to be Moses' address to the people right before they moved toward the Promised Land. The children of Israel have been delivered from slavery in Egypt, led by the cloud by day and fire by night, taken care of on the journey, wandered in the wilderness for 40 years due to unbelief, and received the law to govern them. Moses only has a little time left as their leader, and he gathers them to repeat and remember. At this pivotal point of season change, Moses calls for them to... remember, thank, and recommit.

Quite honestly, as I am writing this chapter, I face a season change. Beloved ones, you should know they are a constant part of living. My FAITHFUL COMPANION was so sweet to call me

to stop .... remember... and thank today. Apparently I needed a
Deuteronomy moment. Because when I stopped to remember
and thank, I found the last part.... committing to obedience
in this new season... to be an easy and obvious choice. For in
looking back, I find these unmistakeable keepsakes of His
FAITHFULNESS and my heart warms with the memories of
how the LOVER OF MY SOUL revealed Himself in that previous
season. Then I exhale and say, "Well of course, BELOVED,
...whatever you think this next season should be. Your UNDYING
LOVE and ROCK SOLID FAITHFULNESS will be there, too. I can
exhale... even in the face of the unknown." As David said at the
end of his declaration of his GREAT SHEPHERD's care...

Psalm 23: 6-
*"Surely goodness and lovingkindness will follow me all the
days of my life, and I will dwell in the house of the LORD
forever."*

I also want to be sure my Deuteronomy moments become
Chronicles for my beloved children and grandchildren. The
purpose of First and Second Chronicles was to trace the history
of FAITHFUL GOD's dealings with His people... to share stories
of the past with a new generation to give them hope and wisdom
for the future... to assure them that NEVER CHANGING GOD...
WAS THERE, IS THERE, and WILL BE THERE! If I were sitting
across from you right now, my dear one, I would take your face
in my hands and look deep in your eyes and tell you that not only
was ETERNAL GOD present in every season of Elijah's life and
every season of Moses' journey with the children of Israel, but

the GREAT I AM has also been present and revealing Himself in every season of my life. I would assure you with all the passion and conviction I could muster that the TREASURE will be with you as well... in every season... I promise. And I would appeal to you not to miss Him... oh don't miss the PEARL OF GREAT PRICE. He literally died to draw you close and reveal His GREATNESS and COMPASSION and WITHNESS to you.

So if you don't know me personally, I hope you will be patient with the next few pages as I open up my scrapbook to share with you Who He has shown Himself to be in some of my seasons. Time and time again when I was completely overwhelmed by my circumstances, my responsibilities, my own weakness, my fears ... I ran. I ran to the ROCK THAT IS HIGHER THAN I... and I crumbled. Time after time, I begged the ALL KNOWING ONE for relief, release, rescue, resources, restitution, direction, change, ... and sometimes He gave those things. But every time... GOD gave GOD... and I exhaled. The strangest thing happened as I soaked in each newly revealed characteristic of MY BELOVED. Those things I was asking for and those circumstances I so desperately needed to change seemed to fade in significance and bow in submission to the PRESENCE of the NAME ABOVE ALL NAMES and the reality of His WITHNESS.

So here are just a few glimpses from my keepsake journal of the seasons and chapters of my life. He is so much MORE THAN WORDS...

Family Seasons (chapter subtitle.. Releasing Control to Find FAITHFUL LOVE)

- A little background- At the time of this writing,

I am a daughter, sister, aunt, wife, mother, and Marmee (grandmother). I am also a recovering perfectionist control freak (yes, this is actually me better). Those family roles overshadowed with my penchant for control gave an amazing backdrop for transformation through His presence. My inability to control everything about my family and everything about the struggles they encountered was truly... a blessing. Though I have to be honest and say that I didn't usually see or treat this "out of control" status as a blessing. Quite honestly, I wailed about each one. I wailed when...

- The husband GOD truly gifted me with was the absolute opposite from me and made decisions or acted in ways I didn't understand.
- The two beautiful daughters I am humbled to call mine struggled with school or life or people or anything at all, when they weren't chosen or accepted or rewarded just how I liked, when they were hurting or scared or stepping out toward a new season themselves.
- The precious, Godly heritage-giving parents and in-laws I was undeservedly given needed their children to slow down and lovingly exchange places with them by walking them home through elder care or release to glory.
- My heartbeat on feet, otherwise known as my grandchildren, faced threats to their well-being beginning in the womb with a scary test result

and continuing into a world that seemed to suddenly (though I know it wasn't sudden) lose all moral compass.

- And in my wailing, GOD revealed Himself to be...
  - FAITHFUL AND TRUE
  - SOURCE OF PEACE
  - WRITER OF MY CHILDREN'S STORY
  - TRUSTWORTHY- THE ONE I AM TO TRUST
  - GIVER OF THE GIFT OF SOLITUDE
  - HE WHO LOVINGLY HEDGES IN
  - ABLE TO ACCOMPLISH MORE FOR MY CHILDREN IN A MOMENT THAN I CAN IN A LIFETIME
  - HE WHO TELLS ME, "I WILL NEVER LEAVE YOU OR FORSAKE YOU."
  - HE WHO CALLS ME NOT TO FIX- MYSELF, OTHERS, MY CIRCUMSTANCES, MY KIDS- BUT TO FIX MY EYES ON HIM
  - CHANGELESS
  - HE WHO REMAINS
  - MAGNIFICENT HEALER
  - GOD WHO DOESN'T FORGET- GOD OF GENERATIONAL PROMISE
  - HE WHO REIGNS SO NO FEAR
  - ABUNDANTLY PRESENT IN EVERY DAY AND EVERY CIRCUMSTANCE
  - THERE- HE IS THERE
  - COMFORTER IN THE SHADOWLANDS

- FAITHFUL LOVE
- TRANSCENDING
- STRONGHOLD OF MY LIFE
- CALLER TO AN ETERNAL VIEW
- MORE THAN ENOUGH

In every season of my family, GOD gave GOD... and I exhaled!

Career Seasons- (chapter subtitle.. Finding the IMMOVABLE when Everything is Shaking and You are In Over your Head)

- A little background- Some people figure out what they want to do in their careers while they are in college or in their older years, but I seemed to know from birth I wanted to be a teacher. I never considered doing anything else. My first teacher's desk was a gift from Santa when I was nine years old, and any children from my neighborhood will tell you I bossed them into letting me always be the teacher. The WAYMAKER truly directed my steps and allowed me to be a teacher... and so much more. At this writing, I have had the joy of working with and for children for over 35 years as a teacher, children's ministry director, staff developer, and principal. What an undeserved honor that has been! (If you are reading this and I taught you as a child in school or church or chapel, I hope you know that you will always be a child of my heart... always.)

Truly one of the most rewarding and challenging jobs I ever had was leading an elementary school at a Christian school. I am forever humbled and grateful GOD allowed me the privilege of combining my love for teaching with my heart's cry to point the next generation to JESUS. Who gets to do both?! As much as I absolutely loved my years as principal, I must with full transparency say being a principal was one of the most challenging, in over my head from day one, drive me to JESUS over and over again experiences of my life. Many (ok most) days found me shaking on the inside and on my knees (or face) telling the PARACLETE I didn't know what to do or how to lead or which decision to make or how to fight the enemy .... perhaps He had chosen the wrong person. But the MASTER GIFT GIVER had not made a mistake. All that responsibility and all that uncertainty was ... one of His greatest gifts to me.

- For in the shaking, GOD revealed Himself to be...
  - IMMOVABLE
  - MY AUDIENCE OF ONE... WHO IS ALREADY PLEASED JUST BECAUSE I AM HIS
  - DEFENDER
  - MY STRENGTH AND SONG
  - MY STAY- MY ABILITY TO STAY
  - ALL I WILL EVER NEED TO ACCOMPLISH ALL YOU ARE ASKING OF ME
  - MY SECURITY AND MY SIGNIFICANCE

- THE ANSWER
- MY VISION
- BEST FRIEND INVITING ME TO SIT AT HIS TABLE
- HE WHO CAUSES THE OCEANS TO TUMULT WHEN HE APPEARS...SO NO FEAR
- HE WHO HAS TRAVELED THE ROAD BEFORE ME SO I CAN KNOW IT IS OK
- HE WHO CLOTHES ME IN STRENGTH AND WRAPS ME IN PEACE
- SHEPHERD WHO GOES BEFORE CLEARING THE PATH
- VOICE BEHIND ME SAYING, "THIS IS THE WAY. WALK IN IT."
- GIVER OF WISDOM
- MORE
- THE ANCHOR OF MY SOUL... MY MIND, MY WILL, MY EMOTIONS
- ABOVE ALL
- DEFENDER OF THE CHILDREN
- LIGHT IN THE DARKNESS
- EL SHADDAI... ALL SUFFICIENT ONE
- THE ONE WHO SAYS, "FOLLOW ME."
- OMNI-FACETED TREASURE
- HE WITH WHOM I AM NEVER "TOO MUCH" OR "NOT ENOUGH"

In every season of my career, GOD gave GOD... and I exhaled!

Financial Shaking and Faith Jumping Seasons- (chapter subtitle... Losing the Security You Crave to Find the PEACE You Long For)

- <u>A little background</u>- I confessed to you a few paragraphs ago my issues with control. Have you ever noticed how many of our "issues" show up in our finances? Having "enough" money (whatever that magical number was), having a budget you stick to, having a solid plan for every possible occurrence in the future... to me this equaled being "secure." Now hear me when I say this, I believe we are called as Christians to work hard, live responsibly, pay our bills, and help others. I also believe if we aren't careful, financial security can become an idol and entitlement can become our norm. Sometimes the GIVER OF FAVOR chooses to favor us by flipping our lives upside down. The SOURCE OF REAL SECURITY is really sweet like that!

  One of my most significant life flips began in 2005 when we decided to build a new house. My husband and I had lived in our first house for eighteen years. We now had two teenagers, we were both working and doing well, we prayed about it, and we decided to build a new house and contract it out ourselves. This might be a good place to mention that we didn't really know anything about the costs and foibles of building our own house. The bottom line here is the house grew significantly above the budget, and our current house would not sell. We were holding two houses and two mortgages, and things were just beginning to get scary.

Welcome to the school of the GREAT PROVIDER.... undergraduate level. The first lesson.. "Everything you have is Mine. I gave it to you to steward." Quite honestly, I was so scared I was kind of relieved it belonged to someone else. Then came the first test. We had built a handicap accessible house, and we had a dear friend who was recently handicapped who needed a few months to heal. If this was the house of the MASTER BUILDER, would we trade houses with another family for a few months? Remember I told you sometimes He gives favor by flipping your life and your comfort upside down. We traded. That was the first gift of this season. Yes, it really was a gift to our family in ways that still bless us fifteen years later.

But school wasn't over. We moved back into our house, and for four years we rented our original house and prayed renters would pay on time. Then in 2009, the renters moved out, the house needed work, we had no money, we were hanging over the cliff again... welcome to the school of the GREAT PROVIDER... graduate level. As Alan hung from a ladder trying to paint the outside of the house and I was at home crying to the OWNER OF IT ALL that we didn't have enough money to steward both houses, the GREAT

COMMUNICATOR told us both that He wanted us to open a home for women who didn't have anywhere else to go. I mentioned to Him (ever so reverently) that the women He was asking us to help had no money, and neither did we. He had told me before to jump and see if He didn't catch me, but this seemed to have free-falling written all over it. But the AUTHOR OF FAITH had spoken, so we jumped. The Blair House opened in 2009.

We knew nothing about running a home for hurting women. We didn't know where the money would come from most of the time. Sometimes it was an anonymous donation, sometimes a local ministry helped us, sometimes the women paid, sometimes we paid it ourselves... bottom line... HE WHO OWNS THE CATTLE ON A THOUSAND HILLS somehow allowed us to own both those houses for fourteen years. To this day, I cannot tell you how that happened. I can tell you that when it was all over... I sobbed with gratitude. I was so grateful for His provision, so grateful for the many miraculous ways He used both houses, so grateful for how He transformed the faith walk of me and Alan and our girls in those years, so grateful for the continuing work of the house through one of the residents who now runs the shelter, so grateful for the gifts of lifelong friendship He gave us with some of the women, so grateful He showed us His true heart for the hurting and the formerly entitled (me), and most grateful for the life-flipping favor that was the secret ingredient to release and true SECURITY.

In the shaky jumping, GOD revealed Himself to be...
- GIVER OF FAVOR... EVEN IF IT HURTS
- OWNER OF IT ALL
- HE WHO CALLS ME TO JUMP AND PROMISES TO CATCH
- HAPPY TO ADVOCATE FOR ME
- CREATOR OF SOMETHING OUT OF NOTHING
- HE WHO DANCES WITH ME ON CLIFFS WHEN FEAR STALKS..JUST LOOK IN MY EYES AND DON'T LOOK DOWN...I WILL LEAD
- MY ONLY SECURITY
- HE WHO SAYS, "LOVELY," WHEN I SAY "BROKEN"
- MY SUPPLY
- FEAR ZAPPER
- CAPTAIN OF THE HOST OF THE LORD
- THE GREAT I AM
- CENTER OF IT ALL... MAJESTY IN THE MIDDLE OF THE MESS
- ADONAI- LORD AND MASTER
- HE TO WHOM I DON'T HAVE TO HIDE OR DIVULGE ANYTHING BECAUSE HE ALREADY KNOWS
- THE SAME... REGARDLESS
- HE WHOSE PURPOSE IS UNCHANGEABLE
- JEHOVAH-NISSI- MY BANNER WHEN CAUGHT BEHIND ENEMY LINES
- AMAZING PROVIDER- SPLITTER OF THE LOAVES

AND FISHES
- GOD OF THE IMPOSSIBLE
- MY PORTION AND MY PRIZE
- MY ESCAPE

In every season of our financial struggle and faith jump, GOD gave GOD... and I exhaled!

Invisible Seasons (chapter subtitle- Discovering TRUE WORTH in Abandoning Your Resume and Relinquishing Your Search)
- <u>A little background</u>- I am going to be very transparent with you and tell you that I struggled with what to call the season I want to tell you about next. I think it is difficult to write this one because I am in the midst of this season... do I call it a quiet season, do I call it retirement (though I hate that word), do I call it middle age (though I would have to live to be 114 if this is the middle)... invisible seems to have a negative connotation? I chose invisible because I think we have seasons where we struggle with feeling invisible at all ages... when we are young and single and everyone is getting married, when we are young parents and our world is anything but quiet and fully sacrificial, when we are divorced or widowed or childless or jobless or whatever everyone else is not, when we are hurting or grieving or sick or in crisis, or when the LORD OF ALL COMPASSION just calls us aside for a little while. A little over a year ago, I felt the SEER OF THE INVISIBLE was telling me to get involved in His invisible work...

ministering to those who feel invisible. When I told Him I didn't know what to say to them, He showed me that the KNOWER OF HEARTS wanted them to know that they were not invisible, but seen and held close to His heart. He wanted them to know that their pain was felt and grieved, and that their needs were recognized and met. I loved the message. I wasn't quite as excited when I realized I was entering just such a season.

I have already told you I am a recovering control freak with security issues so I might as well tell you my achilles heel when it comes to worth. I think we all have one. Some of us rely on relationships for worth and find ourselves constantly searching for that perfect relationship or friend group or community to finally make us feel whole. Some of us, like me, have our worth all twisted up in our performance. Our quest for wholeness seems to revolve around success, reputation, position, and achievement. I have to be honest and say I really thought performance-based worth was something I had left in my young adulthood... until the ONE WHO KNOWS BEST called me to a time alone to rest and be with Him. Facing "retirement" seemed to sound like the end of purpose season instead of the beautiful call to intimacy and TRUE WORTH that He intended. It took me a minute (or maybe a year) to realize, the GREAT WOOER OF MY SOUL was untangling and freeing and gifting with Himself all over again. He knows so much better than

I know what I need. He knows what you need, too, in this "invisible season." He is trying to give you Himself. The aroma of His DIVINE PRESENCE and the masterful way He is the KNOWER OF MY FRAME BETTER THAN I KNOW MYSELF has just left me... awed... and so very grateful to be His ... in every season.

- In the relinquishing, GOD has revealed Himself to be...
  - TRUE WORTH
  - AUTHOR OF IDENTITY
  - FREE-ER FROM ENDLESS, ENTANGLING, EMPTY, DISAPPOINTING PERFORMANCE
  - SOURCE OF TRUTH
  - REWARDER
  - HE WHOSE SIGNATURE IS ON MY SOUL
  - HE WHO IS INTIMATELY INVOLVED IN MY MOMENTS
  - NEARNESS THAT HEALS, HIDES, HOLDS, AND PROTECTS
  - HE WHO BESTOWS HIMSELF
  - INTERCESSOR...KNOWER OF THE MIND AND WILL OF GOD
  - FAIRER THAN....
  - CALLER TO AND GIVER OF REST
  - HE WHOSE PROMISE IS EQUAL TO HIS PRESENCE
  - GOD OF DETOX...DETOXING ME PHYSICALLY, EMOTIONALLY, MENTALLY, AND SPIRITUALLY
  - WAYMAKER

- COMFORTER
- HELPER
- LIFEGIVER
- CLOSEST COMPANION
- PROTECTOR
- GIVER OF PURPOSE
- GOOD... SO VERY GOOD
- ATTENTIVE TO EACH DETAIL
- SO VERY PERSONAL
- FAITHFUL THROUGH ALL SEASONS
- CARRIER
- REMEMBERING
- ALWAYS SEEING AND LOVING
- RESTORING

In this season that may seem invisible, GOD is giving GOD... and I am truly exhaling!

Precious ones, thank you for letting an old lady reminisce through just a few of the keepsakes of her BELOVED's faithfulness. I am so grateful all these years He didn't give me all the things I asked for but instead gave me SO MUCH MORE. In every season, GOD gives GOD... and I exhale. This has left me awed and speechless. But what leaves me just undone and the truth for which I am even more grateful is that He desires to bestow Himself not only on me but also on my beloved children and grandchildren. Because of His unflinching character, everything He is to me He will also be to you... and so much MORE.

2 Corinthians 1:3-4 says,

"Blessed be the God and Father of our Lord Jesus Christ, the Father of mercies and God of all comfort, Who comforts us in all our affliction so that we will be able to comfort those who are in any affliction with the comfort with which we ourselves are comforted by God."

I don't know what season you are currently walking, but I do know how the FATHER OF MERCIES AND GOD OF ALL COMFORT has met me. And I do know He literally died to meet you... today... in this season. Take a minute and go slowly through some of my keepsakes (the capitalized names and characteristics in the book so far). Declare to the KING OF YOUR HEART that He is each of those to you. Turn your face toward Him in this season, and let His MAGNITUDE dwarf the issues, His COMPASSION quell the hurt, and His PRESENCE usher in rest.

<u>*Hold Me, Jesus*</u>
by Rich Mullins

Well, sometimes my life just don't make sense at all
When the mountains look so big,
And my faith just seems so small

So hold me, Jesus,
Cause I'm shaking like a leaf
You have been King of my glory
Won't You be my Prince of Peace

And I wake up in the night and feel the dark
It's so hot inside my soul
I swear there must be blisters on my heart

So hold me, Jesus,
Cause I'm shaking like a leaf
You have been King of my glory
Won't You be my Prince of Peace

Surrender don't come natural to me
I'd rather fight you for something
I don't really want
Than to take what you give that I need
And I've beat my head against so many walls
Now I'm falling down, I'm falling on my knees

And the Salvation Army band is playing this hymn
And Your grace rings out so deep
It makes my resistance seem so thin

So hold me, Jesus,
Cause I'm shaking like a leaf
You have been King of my glory
Won't You be my Prince of Peace

You have been King of my glory
Won't You be my Prince of Peace [23]

Chapter Thirteen:

Wooing and Waiting

When I read the "glory encounters" of Moses, Elijah, Isaiah, and Paul I must admit I find myself pretty jealous.... until I read the whole story. Moses had His encounter with UNFATHOMABLE GLORY while leading through the desert a large group of people who quickly questioned his leadership and his GOD the minute his back was turned. I am pretty sure the day to day reality of that job was anything but glamorous. Elijah encountered the VOICE LIKE NO OTHER when he was running, broken, and ready to die. I am convinced the events that led him to that moment were not day after day of happy encounters. Isaiah's life and country were in a time of leadership change and scary uncertainty when he saw ALL POWERFUL GOD. Paul was going full force in the wrong direction when ALL SEEING GOD blinded him that he might really see. The point I am trying to make here is that we all love to tell stories of glorious encounters and personal transformation... after we have been transformed. But in the midst of the transformation when life is reeling and people are complaining and things aren't working, some days we might just wonder where ALL KNOWING GOD is or worse yet begin to believe closeness with the ALMIGHTY isn't for us.

Precious ones, let me encourage you. The situations you now face that feel like endless, purposeless waiting may actually be the LOVER OF YOUR SOUL wooing you to His heart and His presence. Please don't miss the call to TRUE INTIMACY! Do you remember the story I told you in the last chapter about opening the house for women and all the glorious things the GREAT PROVIDER revealed Himself to be in that faith jump? What I didn't mention was that for fourteen years I begged MIRACLE WORKING GOD for release. Fourteen years.

2 Peter 3:8-9-
"But do not let this one fact escape your notice, beloved, that with the Lord one day is like a thousand years, and a thousand years like one day. The Lord is not slow about His promise, as some count slowness, but is patient toward you, not wishing for any to perish but for all to come to repentance."

The truth I now see is that what I believed to be "nothing is happening" waiting was actually patient wooing on the part of MY BELOVED. I wanted the glory sighting without the risk and without the grief and definitely without the waiting. Isn't there an app for this? No, dear one, there is no app for true intimacy. I wanted a drive-thru solution, but THE TREASURE OF THE AGES wanted to reveal His GREAT WORTH to me. I wanted to feel instantly better. THE AUTHOR OF LOVE wanted real communion with me. With me!!! The reality still leaves me speechless. He

wants that with you, too. I love how Paul E. Miller describes
it in *A Praying Life,* "The waiting that is the essence of faith
provides the context for relationship. Faith and relationship are
interwoven in dance. Everyone talks now about how prayer is
relationship, but often what people mean is having warm fuzzies
with God. Nothing wrong with warm fuzzies, but relationships
are far richer and more complex." [24]

So what does it look like to have a deep relationship with
ALMIGHTY GOD? Our earthly analogies seem so weak, but for
the sake of trying to understand, let's look at marriage to help
explain. As of this writing, I have had the joy and blessing of
being married to the most amazing man for thirty-four years.
Alan is everything I am not and truly the better part of us. I am
forever grateful GOD gave him to me, and he is the love of my
life. Though we are fully human and some days are better than
others, I would like to believe after thirty-four years we have
true intimacy with each other. How did that happen? It began
with a commitment to one another as we became husband and
wife. Similarly our relationship with the ETERNAL BRIDEGROOM
begins when we receive JESUS, the RECONCILER TO GOD, as our
LORD and SAVIOR. We give Him our lives, and He becomes our
LIFE. In that moment, we enter into covenant relationship with
our ONE AND ONLY.

Can you imagine my relationship with Alan if after our
wedding day, I only spent time with him or talked to him when
I wanted something or on Sundays or when I was in trouble?
What if I thought I knew all there was to know about him or
was afraid to learn more about him? What if I pulled away
when life didn't go as I had expected or he didn't do exactly as I

expected? What if I feared rejection or loss so I wasn't willing to get too close? What if my relationship with him didn't look like other relationships I knew, so I just decided to accept a surface relationship? What if I settled for what I knew and the closeness we had on day one? What a waste of a lifetime of knowing, growing, loving, experiencing, and being together! What a sacrifice of true intimacy! Do you see the correlation here? Why would we ever accept these realities when invited to intimacy with THE EMBODIMENT OF TRUE LOVE?

True intimacy requires risk and surrender. It is choosing to draw near... day after day... in the marvelous, the muddy, and the mundane. It is loyalty that chooses to believe the best... and to wait... when that best isn't immediately apparent. It is clinging in the hard times and facing the unknown together. It is knowing... but discovering. It is comfort that sustains but is never boring and refuses to embrace apathy. It is life-giving and life worthy. It is presence that declares homeness no matter the location or the season. THE KNOWER OF YOUR NAME AND ALL THERE IS TO KNOW OF YOU offers you this intimacy with Himself. What does it look like to reciprocate?

1. <u>Surrender is a great place to start</u>. Often we think peace is on the other side of this circumstance or at the end of this season or whenever _____ happens. Peace, my beloved ones, is not on the other side of this situation. Peace is on the other side of surrender. As I bring my feelings, my circumstances, my concerns, my uncertainties, my desires to MY BELOVED, He assures me He can hold them and reveals Himself

to be my PRINCE OF PEACE. My situation may not immediately change, but I can assure you, His revelation of Himself in the midst of the situation changes me... and I exhale.

2. <u>Come needy</u>. We are trained from an early age to avoid dependence... to stand up and be independent. Yet Kingdom living is upside down living.

Jesus said in Matthew 5:3,
" Blessed are the poor in spirit, for theirs is the kingdom of heaven."

I recently studied this passage, and here is a breakdown of what the CALLER TO FULL DEPENDENCE showed me.

Matthew 5:3–
"Blessed (well off/fortunate, favored with extended grace) are the poor (bent, folded, fully dependent) in spirit (at their very essence), for theirs is (to these childlike, different heirs not understood by the world belongs) the kingdom (rule and reign in the heart) of heaven (love, truth, glory, and grace)."

Come needy and come dependent for... well off/fortunate, and favored with extended grace are the bent, folded, and fully dependent at their very essence. For to these childlike, different heirs not understood by the world belong the rule and reign in the heart of LOVE, TRUTH, GLORY, and GRACE. Never be ashamed to come needy to your BELOVED FATHER. Your full dependence draws Him.

3. <u>Come real and raw</u>. Come with all your real and raw
   pain and all your real and raw questions and draw near.
   You may be shocked to find that in that moment as
   you abandon all the right words and just share your
   true aching heart and soul, He is NEAR. NEARNESS
   THAT HEALS, HIDES, HOLDS, AND PROTECTS will be
   NEARNESS IN ALL THE FULLNESS OF HIS NAME. In
   other words... TRUTH draws near. HOPE draws near.
   HEALER draws near. PROVIDER draws near. Read back
   over all the capitalized names and characteristics and
   declare Him NEAR IN ALL THE FULLNESS OF HIS NAME.

*Jesus said in Matthew 5:4, "Blessed are those who mourn for
they shall be comforted."*

Let's break that one down.

Matthew 5:4-
"Blessed (well off/ fortunate and favored with extended
grace) *are those who mourn* (aching and grieving over
a death so severe it can't be hidden) *, for they shall be
comforted* (called near)."

Come real and raw with your aching and grieving heart
for you will be called near! Isn't it beautiful to know that to
be comforted is to be called near. I picture it like the GREAT
SHEPHERD pulling His most fragile lamb up to His heart for

protection. Real and raw leads to revelation of ourselves and of Him. The COMFORTER is here, and there is relationship and relief!

4. <u>Come day after day after day and season after season after season</u>. Just like intimacy in marriage is forged in the marvelous and the muddy and the mundane, intimacy with our HOLDER OF DAYS is built as we daily come. We come to thank, we come for direction, we come for comfort, we come to understand, we come to mourn, we come to release, we come to ask, we come to hear.... We simply keep coming!!

Matthew 7:7 says,
"Ask, and it will be given to you; seek, and you will find; knock, and it will be opened to you."

The interpretation for this verse is actually "ask and keep on asking", "seek and keep on seeking", "knock and keep on knocking."

Jesus said in Matthew 5:6,
"Blessed are those who hunger and thirst for righteousness, for they shall be satisfied."

Let's break that one down further.

Matthew 5:6–
"Blessed (well off/ fortunate and favored with extended

grace) *are those who hunger and thirst for righteousness* (are those who crave and desire earnestly that which is approved in God's eyes), *for they shall be satisfied* (for they shall be abundantly filled)."

Do you want intimacy with the LOVER OF YOUR SOUL? Then keep coming. He never disappoints. GREAT IMMENSENESS will give you what you need and what you can handle for today. So often, I leave my time with Him with one simple phrase or verse or Name or truth that I meditate on all day... one morsel of His GREATNESS that somehow draws His NEARNESS to my awareness all day. I take that morsel, and I meditate and battle with it all day long. Once during a difficult season HE WHO DANCES WITH ME ON CLIFFS WHEN FEAR STALKS gave me, "Don't look down. Just fix your eyes right here on Me." Once when weariness and discouragement were weighing heavy, He reminded me, "I am your STRENGTH and your SONG." When the responsibilities were stronger than I could handle, I repeated all day, "I give this to the ROCK HIGHER THAN I." I cannot explain it, but as I come day after day and year after year, GOD gives GOD...I fight my fears with the reality of His character... and I exhale... as I am transformed! Waiting becomes wooing as THE GREAT I AM calls me close.

5. And when it is hard, don't run... you are being wooed to come closer. The real mettle of relationships is how they handle hard seasons. Does the challenge drive them closer into an impenetrable togetherness or cause them to turn somewhere else for comfort and relief? Beloved

ones, hard times will come. Take heart. TRANSFORMING
GOD is drawing you close.

2 Corinthians 7:10 says,
" For the sorrow that is according to the will of God produces a
repentance without regret leading to salvation, but the sorrow
of the world produces death."

Let's take a closer look at this scripture.

2 Corinthians 7:10 says,
"For the sorrow (grief, pain, heaviness) *that is according*
to the will of God (agreeable to the will of/ pleases God)
produces (accomplishes) *a repentance* (change of mind,
change in the inner man) *without regret* (about which
no change of mind can take place/ deep conviction/
irrevocable) *leading to salvation* (that which should be the
present possession of all true Christians/ deliverance) *, but*
the sorrow (grief, pain, heaviness) *of the world* (ungodly
multitude, the whole mass alienated from God and hostile
to the cause of God) *produces* (accomplishes) *death* (death/
misery, living death, the loss of that life worthy of the
name)."

Everyone experiences sorrow. It is the result of
the fall of man. But in relationship with HE WHO SAYS
"BEAUTIFUL" WHEN I SAY "BROKEN," sorrow has purpose
and transformational power. If we look again at 2 Corinthians
7:10, we see that the grief, pain, and heaviness that is agreeable

to the will of and pleases GOD accomplishes something. It accomplishes a change of mind and change of the inner man about which no other change of mind can take place... a deep conviction... an irrevocable confidence. This unwavering conviction should be the present possession of every true believer for it is the key to deliverance. But the grief, pain, and heaviness of the ungodly multitude, the whole mass alienated from God and hostile to the cause of God accomplishes death, misery, being among the living dead who have lost the life worthy to even be called life. Do you see the truth, dear one? Sorrow handled the way of the world can leave you literally among the walking dead, but sorrow used to woo you close to the GREAT REDEEMER OF ALL PAIN can make you unshakeable! And about that intimacy...

> **James 1:12 says,**
> *"Blessed is a man who perseveres under trial; for once he has been approved, he will receive the crown of life which the Lord has promised to those who love Him."*

Let's look at this closely to see the promise that comes when we don't run when things are hard.

> **James 1:12 says,**
> *"Blessed* (well off/ fortunate and favored with extended grace) *is a man who perseveres* (endures, bears bravely and calmly) *under trial; for once he has been approved* (proven, tried, tested), *he will receive the crown of life* (knowing HIM) *which the Lord has promised to those who love Him."*

Do you see the connection? The promise to those who surrender, come needy and real and raw, day after day, when sorrow comes and times are hard... the reward...is the crown of knowing Him and loving Him. Knowing Him and loving Him... I believe we call that intimacy. Waiting becomes wooing... and as we draw near, we find Him to be ... MORE THAN WONDERFUL!

More than Wonderful
Written by Lanny Wolfe
Sung by Larnelle Harris and Sandi Patty

He promised us that He would be a counselor
A Mighty God and the Prince of Peace
He promised us that He would be a Father
And that He would love us with a love that would not cease.

Well, I tried Him and I found His promises are true
He's everything He said that He would be.
The finest words I know could not begin to tell
Just what Jesus really means to me.

For He's more wonderful than my mind can conceive
He's more wonderful than my heart can believe
He goes beyond my highest hopes and fondest dreams.
He's everything that my soul ever longed for
Everything that He's promised and so much more
He's more than amazing, more than marvelous
More than miraculous could ever be
He's more than wonderful, that's what Jesus is to me.

I stand amazed when I think that the King of glory
Would come to dwell within the heart of man
Oh, I marvel just to know He really loves me
When I think of who He is, and who I am.

For He's more wonderful than my mind can conceive
He's more wonderful than my heart can believe
He goes beyond my highest hopes and fondest dreams.
He's everything that my soul ever longed for
Everything that He's promised and so much more
He's more than amazing, more than marvelous
More than miraculous could ever be
He's more than wonderful, that's what Jesus is to me.

He's everything that my soul ever longed for
Everything that He's promised and so much more
He's more than amazing (more than amazing)
More than marvelous (that's what my Jesus is)
More than miraculous (that's what my Savior is) could ever be
He's more than wonderful, more than wonderful
That's what Jesus is (that's what Jesus is) to me.
He's more than wonderful to me
(He's wonderful to me)[25]

143

SECTION FOUR:

Taste and See

Psalm 34:8-

"<u>O taste and see that the Lord is good</u>; how blessed is the man who takes refuge in Him!"

Chapter Fourteen:

The Secret

D ear ones, it is time for us to talk about your life. You only get one life... and that life is brief... so how you live it really does matter. Do you ever wonder what's the secret? Is there any real hope or certainty when it comes to getting this little blink of time we call our lives... right? Today's popular message seems to be that you are free to believe, declare yourself to be, and act upon whatever you desire or feel. With this messaging comes the underlying declaration that there is no absolute truth, so decide what is right for you and "go for it." Doesn't that sound so freeing? But without truth, there is no certainty. And without certainty, the ground is always shifting at the whim of my feelings, my control, my circumstances, my performance, my status... shifting ground is anything but freeing. It is terrifying.

But as true believers in JESUS CHRIST, we were promised truth that frees us, an unshakeable kingdom, and certainty in which to stand.

John 8:31-32 says, "So Jesus was saying to those Jews who had believed Him, 'If you continue in My word, then you are truly disciples of Mine; and you will know the truth, and the truth will make you free.'"

Hebrews 12:28-29 states, "Therefore, since we receive a kingdom which cannot be shaken, let us show gratitude by which we may offer to God an acceptable service with reverence and awe; for our God is a consuming fire."

May I ask you a few things about your one brief life, beloved one? I am just wondering ... how free are you? How firm is the ground on which you stand? What is the secret to unshakeable certainty? Do you possess it?

In Romans 5, the GREAT REVEALER OF TRUTH shows us the secret to the certainty we so desperately need if we are going to live a life that truly impacts...

Romans 5:1-2 says, "Therefore, having been justified by faith, we have peace with God through our Lord Jesus Christ, through whom also we have obtained our introduction by faith into this grace in which we stand, and we exult in hope of the glory of God."

According to this passage, certainty starts with our foundation as believers... those who have full and complete salvation through the sacrificial death and resurrecting life of the very SON OF GOD. When we by faith receive JESUS as our own PERSONAL SAVIOR and LORD OF OUR LIFE, He becomes our JUSTIFIER completely conforming us to the standard... so we can stop striving. He also becomes our RECONCILER bringing us back to a peaceful relationship with our FATHER... so we can stop stressing. Through JESUS, we are also introduced to a daily GRACE in which we stand. GRACE ... GOD freely extending Himself reaching toward people because He is disposed to be near them... is based on His UNCHANGING CHARACTER and not ours... so we can stop shaking.

So how do we respond to this UNFATHOMABLE GIFT? We "exult in the hope of the glory of God." What does that mean? Exult means to lift our head confidently and boast. I also like to think of it as doing the happy dance. Hope in scripture is better defined as expecting what is sure or being... certain. Certain in what... certain in the glory... the UNCHANGING WOW of GOD. So when this passage says, "we exult in the hope of the glory of God," it is saying we lift our heads and boast (do the happy dance) in the certainty of the UNCHANGING WOW of GOD.

Lean in, dear ones. Here is the secret to your own personal lifelong unshakeable certainty. Are you ready for the secret to truly living? The unshakeable ground you are looking for that will give you purpose and confidence to live every single day is ... the UNWAVERING and UNSHAKEABLE CHARACTER of ALMIGHTY GOD and the UNFATHOMABLE GRACE that makes Him want to share it with you.

But according to Romans 5, there is MORE. Not only can you be certain of His FLAWLESS CHARACTER, you can also be certain of the DIVINE STORYTELLER's purposes in your life.[26]

Romans 5:3-5 says,
"And not only this, but we also exult in our tribulations,

knowing that tribulation brings about perseverance; and perseverance, proven character; and proven character, hope, and hope does not disappoint, because the love of God has been poured out within our hearts through the Holy Spirit Who was given to us."

In other words, dear ones, embrace the journey even when it is hard, certain of the character of the SUPREME ORCHESTRATOR who wastes nothing. Refuse to shut down and assume the LOVER OF YOUR SOUL is either absent or uncaring. Narrow your eyes to look for the strokes of the DIVINE ARTIST. Ask the TEACHER what PUREST LOVE is trying to accomplish in you, for you, or through you? Trust. If you are feeling hemmed in by a situation or by life itself, trust He is at work. According to this passage, pressure (tribulation) brings about a patient steadfast waiting on His character (perseverance). This waiting and watching brings about transformation (proven character). This transformation brings about more certainty (hope) in the character and purposes of TRUSTWORTHY GOD. This certainty does not disappoint because it is always a HOLY SPIRIT love bath as GOD gives GOD... again.

INDESCRIBABLE LOVE washes over you again and again as you bathe in the certainty of His character and soak in the certainty of His purposes. Somehow you lose yourself and finally find yourself all at the same time. Love does that. You have found the secret.

But there is MORE. The beautiful thing about this newfound certainty is it brings COMFORT for you and ABUNDANT OVERFLOW for others.

2 Corinthians 1:3-4 says, "Blessed be the God and Father of our Lord Jesus Christ, the Father of mercies and God of all comfort, who comforts us in all our affliction so that we will be able to comfort those who are in any affliction with the comfort with which we ourselves are comforted by God."

Do you see the cycle, dear one? As you bathe in the certainty of His character and soak in the certainty of His purposes for your life, your life can't hold the TIDAL WAVE OF LOVE you experience. The overflow engulfs those around you with His LIFE CHANGING LOVE and EVER PRESENT COMFORT. When I began to make a list of names and character traits of GOD several years ago, I expected the list to be a reminder and encouragement for my walk. It has infinitely accomplished that desire. However, perhaps equally revolutionary to my walk was the way the list changed my prayers for others. The GREAT ADVOCATE began to have me pray certain of His names and character traits over people and situations. Somehow praying the certainty of His character and the certainty of His purposes over other people gave me this REPRODUCING BLESSING. As I prayed His name or character over someone else, I was reminded of His GREATNESS and NEARNESS again. My love deepened for both Him and the person for whom I was praying.

Ultimately, precious ones, this is the secret to living a life that matters. We try to make following JESUS so very complicated. He simplified it for us.

Matthew 22:35-40 says, "One of them, a lawyer, asked Him a question, testing Him, 'Teacher, which is the great commandment in the Law?' And He said to him, 'You shall love the LORD your God with all your heart, and with all your soul, and with all your mind.' This is the great and foremost commandment. The second is like it, 'You shall love your neighbor as yourself.' On these two commandments depend the whole Law and the Prophets."

You only have one brief life, dear one. The secret to having the one life you've been given fully fulfill its true purpose is really quite certain and quite simple. Your certain and simple purpose is to love people as a natural overflow of your all consuming love affair with GOD ALMIGHTY...THE BURNING FLAME OF LOVE.

How is that love affair going? We are coming to the end of this letter/ book. I simply must ask you, "Won't you come to the table?"

<u>My Hope is Built on Nothing Less</u>
By Edward Mote

My hope is built on nothing less
Than Jesus' blood and righteousness
I dare not trust the sweetest frame
But wholly lean on Jesus' name

On Christ the solid rock I stand
All other ground is sinking sand
All other ground is sinking sand

When darkness veils his lovely face
I rest on His unchanging grace
In every high and stormy gale
My anchor holds within the veil

His oath, his covenant, his blood
Supports me in the 'whelming flood
When all around my soul gives way
He then is all my hope and stay

On Christ the solid rock I stand
All other ground is sinking sand
All other ground is sinking sand

When He shall come with trumpet sound
Oh may I then in Him be found
Dressed in his righteousness alone
Faultless to stand before the throne

On Christ the solid rock I stand
All other ground is sinking sand
All other ground is sinking sand [27]

Chapter Fifteen:

Come to the Table

Have you ever spent an evening looking at someone else's vacation pictures? You may enjoy hearing the stories and love seeing the joy on their face as they tell them, but nothing compares to taking the vacation yourself. Seeing pictures of a friend standing on the beach is fun, but the enjoyment pales in light of your own personal moment facing the ocean with the sand beneath your feet, the tide gently brushing your ankles, the salt air coming through a gentle breeze, and the sun warming your face. This is your moment... and if you soak it in... it takes your breath away.

Precious ones, I can't tell you how much I have enjoyed sharing with you my... decades long, new every day, more precious than air, reason for living... love story with the EMBODIMENT OF ALL TRUE LOVE. But this is my story. He wants to write yours. Love stories are very personal. Who is JESUS to you... not to your parents or your grandparents or your church or your friends or the world... but who do you say He is?

Jesus posed this question to his disciples in Matthew 16:13-19.

Matthew 16:13-14 says,
"Now when Jesus came into the district of Caesarea Philippi, He was asking His disciples, 'Who do people say that the Son of Man is?' And they said, 'Some say John the Baptist; and others, Elijah; but still others, Jeremiah, or one of the prophets.'"

The Bible is so very relatable. JESUS had caused quite a buzz, and opinions were flying as to His true identity. There were the religious who questioned and debated as if they really wanted to know Who He was, but they really only wanted to prove they were right. There were crowd followers who enjoyed the show and the latest phenomenon but really had no depth of hunger for Who He really claimed to be. There were the bruised and hurting who sometimes hid behind their defenses as He pursued them with compassion.There were His own disciples who were sometimes so distracted by their current circumstance or their own performance that they couldn't really grasp what He was trying to teach. We see these same responses and these same groups today. But the KNOWER OF HEARTS had a deeper question for His true disciples.

Jesus said in Matthew 16:15,
"He said to them, 'But Who do you say that I am?'"

For many years, I worked in a Christian school and interviewed countless potential staff members. I would say in those interviews, "Tell me about your relationship with CHRIST.

How did you come to know Him? Who is He to you today?" Some would talk of parents and grandparents who knew the SAVIOR. Some would mention growing up in church and going to Sunday school. Some would talk of current church attendance and denominational affiliations. Some would tell how they served at their church. Those were interesting conversations, but they didn't answer what I was really asking. I wanted to know, "Who is He to you?"

Jesus' question to His disciples went straight to the heart of the matter... straight to their hearts. He wanted to know... Who... am...I... to...you? That really is the heart of the matter, dear one. When the SEER TO THE SOUL looks you in the eyes and asks, "Who do you say I am?" Ultimately, the opinion and stance of others means very little at that moment. How do you answer that question, dear one? Who is He to you?

Matthew 16:16 continues the discourse,
"Simon Peter answered, 'You are the Christ, the Son of the living God.'"

Beloved, I wish I could have been an eyewitness at that moment. Was there a pause? Did the other disciples look puzzled? Did Peter just blurt out the answer because he couldn't hold it in any longer? We don't really know all that, but we do know Peter, who walked every day with JESUS, knew exactly Who He was! He may not be able to explain all the details of the plan, but one thing Peter knew for himself...JESUS was the PROMISED SAVIOR, the MESSIAH, the VERY SON OF GOD. And that changed everything!

New identity/name, new purpose, new power, new calling... knowing JESUS as SAVIOR and KING changed everything...

Matthew 16:17-19 says,
"And Jesus said to him, 'Blessed are you, Simon Barjona, because flesh and blood did not reveal this to you, but My Father Who is in heaven. I also say to you that you are Peter, and upon this rock I will build My church; and the gates of Hades will not overpower it. I will give you the keys of the kingdom of heaven; and whatever you bind on earth shall have been bound in heaven, and whatever you loose on earth shall be loosed in heaven.'"

But that was just the beginning...

Paul prayed for his dear children in Ephesians 3:14-17a,
"For this reason I bow my knees before the Father, from Whom every family in heaven and on earth derives its name, that He would grant you, according to the riches of His glory, to be strengthened with power through His Spirit in the inner man, so that Christ may dwell in your hearts through faith;"

Faith would begin the journey, but there was MORE...

Ephesians 3:17b-21 continues the prayer,
"and that you, being rooted and grounded in love, may be able to comprehend (to lay hold of, seize) *with all the saints* (that includes you, dear one) *what is the breadth and length and height and depth, and to know* (to know through personal

experience) *the love of Christ which surpasses knowledge, that you may be filled up to all the fullness of God. Now to Him Who is able to do far more abundantly beyond all that we ask or think, according to the power that works within us, to Him be the glory in the church and in Christ Jesus to all generations forever and ever. Amen."*

There would be UNSHAKEABLE LOVE... there would be BOUNDLESS LOVE... there would be LOVE THAT SURPASSES HEAD KNOWLEDGE...there would be FILLING AND OVERFLOWING LOVE... there would be ABUNDANTLY MORE THAN WE CAN ASK OR THINK....there would be GLORIOUS DAY AFTER DAY, MOMENT AFTER MOMENT, SEASON AFTER SEASON, GENERATION AFTER GENERATION GOD...giving Himself ...to those who would simply come to the table.

You see, beloved ones, EAGER TO REVEAL HIMSELF GOD has spread before us the banquet table of His ABSOLUTE AWESOMENESS and INEXPLICABLE TSUNAMI OF LOVE. MARVELOUS GRACE engraved the invitation with the very blood of HIS ONLY SON. INTIMATE GOD encourages you to partake.

Faith comes to the table.[28]

Please don't settle for the scraps of what others tell you about Him. Please don't believe the lie that the table is just for the Bible scholars and essay writers. Faith simply comes to the table and asks. Faith trusts the GREAT TEACHER living inside and comes to the table.

Jeremiah 33:2-3 says,
"Thus says the LORD who made the earth, the LORD who formed it to establish it, the LORD is His name, 'Call to Me and I will answer you, and I will tell you great and mighty things, which you do not know.'"

Jesus promised in John 16:13-15,
"But when He, the Spirit of truth, comes, He will guide you into all the truth; for He will not speak on His own initiative, but whatever He hears, He will speak; and He will disclose to you what is to come. He will glorify Me, for He will take of Mine and will disclose it to you. All things that the Father has are Mine; therefore I said that He takes of Mine and will disclose it to you."

The table is for all His children. The ULTIMATE GUIDE lives inside. Come hungry, come often, come expectant, come eager... come to the table for yourself.

Don't think He has to teach you just like everyone else. The INTRICATE CREATOR designed you. I am pretty sure He knows your learning style. When my DEAREST SAVIOR reveals Himself to me, I write in journals, make lists, plan lessons that may or may not ever be taught, and study words. He sometimes reveals Himself to me through books and songs and conversations. I have a dear artistic friend named Katie who loves to take walks and talk with Him. He sometimes reveals Himself to her through hymns and sunsets and intricate parts of nature I would overlook. When her DEAREST SAVIOR reveals Himself to Katie, she comes home and paints amazing pictures or creates masterpieces reflecting His love and glory. I have another dear friend named Tammy with the most passionate, child-like heart. Like me and like Katie, she loves the Word of GOD and studies it deliberately. LOVER OF THE CHILDLIKE HEART sometimes reveals Himself to Tammy through music she plays loudly or while dancing like nobody's watching while walking on the beach. When her DEAREST SAVIOR reveals Himself to Tammy, she writes children's Bible studies and makes note-cards all replete with stickers and bright colors. I have a mentor named Scott who is confined to a wheelchair and spends hours studying, journaling, and pursuing his GREATEST DELIGHT through the lens of his camera and the end of his pen. When his DEAREST SAVIOR and FRIEND IN THE FIRE reveals Himself to Scott, he writes blogs and sermons that encourage many to come close. My husband, Alan, is an airplane mechanic who loves to listen to sermons, watch teachings online, and go on bike rides to pray and meditate. His DEAREST SAVIOR often reveals Himself to him through word pictures about machines and airplanes and glimpses of His glory in nature. He responds by excitedly telling others what He is learning and listening intently to what they have discovered.

Katie, Tammy, Scott, Alan, and I are each created very differently. We each experience His revelations of Himself through different modalities. But we all gratefully embrace Him as our ONE AND ONLY SAVIOR. We all hunger to know and love OUR BELOVED more... so we ask. We all study His Word like we are looking for buried treasure, and cling to the certainty of His UNFAILING CHARACTER. We all watch for the moves of the DIVINE ARTIST and SOVEREIGN STORYTELLER in each nuance

of life and trust the GRAND CHOREOGRAPHER is working for
our good... even when the evidence isn't immediately evident.
In short... we all come to the table. We all have moments
of fear and moments of doubt. We all stumble and fall and
sometimes struggle to get back on our feet. We all have days we
fail miserably. We have all been journeying with our CLOSEST
FRIEND for decades, and the one thing we have learned is to get
back up (or crawl if you have to) and come to the table. Truly my
hope in writing this book for all of you was to remind you that
the table was set and to perhaps leave you just a little hungry.

Will you humor me just one more time, and go back through
the book and read the capitalized names and characteristics? He
desires to be each of these in your life? Precious ones, He is all
this and SO MUCH MORE! GOD gives GOD... we can all exhale!
At the beginning of this book, I told you I was primarily writing
this as a heart letter to my children and grandchildren and to
all my children and grandchildren in the faith (all of those little
children now grown who I had the joy of teaching in school, in
church, in chapel, and around my table). I so desperately wanted
all of you to know... GOD is REAL, GOD is WORTHY, and GOD is
WORTH IT ALL! I promise!

Please know how desperately I love you all. My heart joins
Paul in praying for you...

Philippians 1:3-11 says,
*"I thank my God in all my remembrance of you, always offering
prayer with joy in my every prayer for you all, in view of your
participation in the gospel from the first day until now. For
I am confident of this very thing, that He who began a good*

work in you will perfect it until the day of Christ Jesus. For it is only right for me to feel this way about you all, because I have you in my heart, since both in my imprisonment and in the defense and confirmation of the gospel, you all are partakers of grace with me. For God Is my witness, how I long for you all with the affection of Christ Jesus. And this I pray, that your love may abound still more and more in real knowledge and all discernment, so that you may approve the things that are excellent, in order to be sincere and blameless until the day of Christ; having been filled with the fruit of righteousness which comes through Jesus Christ, to the glory and praise of God."

God Gives God... and I Exhale

BIBLIOGRAPHY

Throughout
- *NASB Giant Print Reference Bible: Personal Size: New American Standard Bible.* Grand Rapids, MI: Zondervan Pub. House, 2000.
- Bible lexicon. Accessed August 2, 2021. https://biblehub. com/lexicon/.

Chapter One: Have We Lost Our AWE
1. Tozer, A.W. Essay. In *The Knowledge of the Holy*, 1. New York, NY: HarperCollins Publishers, 1978.

Chapter Two: Amazed by the Enormity of His Character
2. Wilkin, Jen. *None like Him: 10 Ways God Is Different from Us (and Why That's a Good Thing).* Wheaton, IL: Crossway, 2016.
3. Wilkin, Jen. *In His IMAGE: 10 Ways God Calls Us to Reflect His Character.* Wheaton, IL: Crossway, 2018.

Chapter Three: Wonderstruck by the Beauty of His Ways
4. McGee, Robert S. *The Search for Significance.* Nashville: Thomas Nelson, 2003.
5. 1707. *When I Survey the Wondrous Cross.* Isaac Watts.
6. Wikipedia contributors, "Repentance," *Wikipedia, The Free Encyclopedia*, https://en.wikipedia.org/w/index. php?title=Repentance&oldid=1036498388 (accessed August 2, 2021).

Chapter Four: More Wonderstruck by the Beauty of His Ways
7. 1917. *The Love of God.* Meir Ben Isaac Nehoria.

Chapter Five: Enraptured by the Reality of His Presence
8. 1913. *In the Garden.* Charles Austin Miles.
9. Voskamp, Ann. Essay. In *The Greatest Gift: Unwrapping the FULL Love Story of Christmas*, 234. Carol Stream, IL: Tyndale House Publishers, Inc., 2014.

Chapter Six: A Cry for Intimacy
10. Fiddell, Miles. 2021. "Trusting God's Heart." Transcript of sermon delivered at Auburn Community Church, March 22, 2021.
11. McGee, Robert S. *The Search for Significance.* Nashville: Thomas Nelson, 2003.
12. Voskamp, Ann. *ONE Thousand GIFTS; A Dare to Live Fully Right Where You Are.* Nashville: Thomas Nelson, 2011.

Chapter Seven: The Living Love Letter... Love Has a Name
13. Moore, Beth. *Discovering God's Purpose for Your Life.* Houston, TX: Living Proof Ministries, 2004.
14. Bright, Vonette. *Daily Wisdom from God: 365 Real-Life Stories that will Give You Peace, Hope, and Joy.* Peachtree City, GA: FC&A Publishing, 2017.

Chapter Eight: A TREASURE Greater than the Blessings We Seek
15. Miller, Paul E. Essay. In *A Praying Life: Connecting with God in a Distracting World*, 67. Colorado Springs, CO: NavPress, 2017.
16. Lewis, C.S. 1942. "The Weight of Glory." Transcript of sermon delivered at the Church of St. Mary the Virgin, June 8, 1942.

Chapter Nine: The Blessing
17. Batterson, Mark. Essay. In *Double Blessing: How to Get It, How to Give It*, 43–50. Colorado Springs, CO: Multnomah, an imprint of Random House, 2019.

Chapter Ten: Show Me Your GLORY

18. 1741. *Hallelujah Chorus*. George Frideric Handel.
19. Piper, John. 2002. "Subjected to Futility in Hope." Transcript of sermon delivered at Bethlehem Baptist Church, April 28 and May 5, 2002.

Chapter Eleven: In Every Season

20. Keller, Phillip. *A Shepherd Looks at Psalm 23*. London: Pickering and Inglis, 1976.
21. Schneider, Cynthia. *FROM Passover TO PENTECOST*. S.l.: Charisma House, 2021.
22. 1905, *His Eye is On the Sparrow*. Civilla Durfee Martin.

Chapter Twelve: Keepsakes of Faithfulness

23. Richard Mullins, "Hold Me, Jesus." Released 1986. Track 4 on *Simply Rich Mullins*.

Chapter Thirteen: Wooing and Waiting

24. Miller, Paul E. Essay. In *A Praying Life: Connecting with God in a Distracting World*, 192. Colorado Springs, CO: NavPress, 2017.
25. Sandi Patti and Larnelle Harris, "More Than Wonderful." Released 1983. Track 8, *More Than Wonderful*, Impact Records. Written by Lanny Wolfe.

Chapter Fourteen: The Secret

26. Miller, Paul E. Essay. In *A Praying Life: Connecting with God in a Distracting World*, 203-204. Colorado Springs, CO: NavPress, 2017.
27. 1834, *My Hope is Built on Nothing Less*. Edward Mote.

Chapter Fifteen: Come to the Table

28. Grubb, Norman P. Essay. In *Touching the Invisible: Living by Unseen Realities*, 84. Fort Washington, PA: CLC Publications, 2016.

Made in the USA
Columbia, SC
14 December 2021

51412576R00091